Advance Praise for
Your Crocodile has Arrived

King is one of those **intrepid** female travel writers who … stumbles into dangerous, disturbing and terribly odd situations. **Always worth the read.**

— Tim Cahill, Author, *Jaguars Ripped My Flesh* and *Lost in My Own Backyard*

::::::

King's curiosity is contagious —whether she's visiting a shrine to Buddha's tooth, undergoing shamanic surgery, or crashing a convention of flying saucer sighters … King is a wonderful guide and companion. Her tales glow with **wit, warmth, and a sense of wonder.**

— Jeff Greenwald, Author, *Shopping for Buddhas* and *The Size of the World*

::::::

A super follow-up to *Lost, Kidnapped, Eaten Alive!* … **marvelously entertaining** and often **profoundly moving.**

— Linda Watanabe McFerrin, Author, *Namako, The Hand of Buddha,* and *Dead Love*

Full of **whimsy and good humor** ... you'll be happy
you were there with her.

— Larry Habegger, Executive Editor, Travelers' Tales

::::::

Enchanting ... Each story reads like a veritable treasure
in the Cabinets of Curiosity King deftly describes ...
an antidote to the streak of snark in so much modern
travel writing.

— Phil Cousineau, Author, *The Art of Pilgrimage, The
Book of Roads,* and *The Painted Word*

::::::

Quirky humor, lively style, clear voice ... Get ready for
a can't-put-it-down read.

— Diane LeBow, Ph.D., Author of the forthcoming
book, *My Dinner with Terrorists, and other tales of a
traveling woman*

::::::

Every chapter is a gem! **You'll want to pack up and go**
in search of adventure.

— Julie Freestone, journalist and co-author with Rudi
Raab of *Stumbling Stone*

Wry, informative, and often tender ... King gracefully reminds us about one of the best reasons to travel: to become a better person. This book is definite kindling for wanderlust.

— Jennica Peterson, former senior editor at *Afar* magazine and lifelong traveler

:::::

A **marvelously descriptive** writer who puts you smack in the middle of all her adventures.

— Pamela Feinsilber, editor; culture critic; former Travel Editor, *San Francisco* magazine

:::::

King's stories illustrate the **wonder and diversity** of the world, and why travel is always alluring—even when events don't turn out perfectly.

— Jill K. Robinson, freelance journalist

:::::

King is a **gutsy traveler** and a true Renaissance woman. It's one amazing book!

— Camille Cusumano, Author, *Wilderness Begins at Home* and *Tango, an Argentine Love Story*

King's account of giant worms is **delightfully humorous.**

— Ginny Prior, Radio show host and "The Happy Wanderer" columnist

::::

King drops little bombs of wisdom that go far beyond just travel. And **you'll find yourself cheering** from the sidelines, "Just do it, Laurie! **Do it now!**"

— Bradley Charbonneau, Author, *Every Single Day*

::::

King teaches us how even adventurous menu selections can create **vivid memories** —as long as they are made by your traveling companions, thereby allowing you to pass on the witchetty grubs, emu filets, and crocodile tail and settle for something more mundane and vaguely familiar such as "Lamb in the Log."

— Dick Jordan, Publisher, Tales Told From The Road

::::

Relentlessly inquisitive.

— Michael Shapiro, Author, *A Sense of Place: Travel Writers Talk About Their Craft, Lives, and Inspiration*

I thought I'd give "Haggis Hunter" a wee peek and read the whole book later, but once I started, there was no turning back. **Wonderful evocative writing, irresistible narrative voice**.

— Philip O. Chomak, Author, *Beside the Point: Close Encounters in the Global Classroom*

::::::

I couldn't stop reading … **elegantly and perceptively written**, intelligent and entertaining.

— *Wanda Hennig, Author, Cravings: A Zen-inspired memoir about sensual pleasures, freedom from dark places, and living and eating with abandon*

::::::

Your Crocodile Has Arrived opens with the author hanging 630 feet above the streets of Auckland on the Sky Tower's SkyWalk. Brave author. I too experienced the SkyWalk, but from the safety of the high-level restaurant, where I cowered in fear. The rest of *Crocodile* is just as **brave**, just as **bold**.

— Jules Older, Author, *Death by Tartar Sauce: A Travel Writer Encounters Gargantuan Gators, Irksome Offspring, Murderous Mayonnaise & True Love*

"The Dumpling Men of Taipei" is, like the delicious pleated delights King describes, "a perfect little gem" filled with **sharp and observant writing**. (How *do* they get the soup inside? Now I know.)

— Kimberley Lovato, Author, *Unique Eats & Eateries: San Francisco*

:::::

King's **adventurous spirit** and taste for the unusual make her an **ideal guide** to some of the lesser-known wonders of the world.

— Thomas Swick, Author, *The Joys of Travel: And Stories That Illuminate Them*

:::::

Combines the exuberance and gutsy-ness of youthful travel with the tempered wisdom of maturity.... To see and portray **beauty and sorrow in the same lens** is King's gift.

— Joanna Biggar, Author, *That Paris Year*

King brings **insight, humor and thoughtfulness** to her very tasty writing.

Gayle Keck, Travel and food writer, proprietor of FoodTourFinder.com

::::::

Takes the reader on a **journey of heart and mind** to unexpected destinations, challenges and revelations.

— Eddy Ancinas, Author, *Tales from Two Valleys: Squaw Valley and Alpine Meadows*

::::::

Original and funny … riveting **yet slightly disturbing** — I really enjoyed the read!

— Lisa Alpine, Author, *Wild Life: Travel Adventures of a Worldly Woman* and *Exotic Life*

::::::

King's powerful piece on saving wild elephants is **a moment you should not miss** —even if it hurts.

— Natalie Lefevre, Editor, Ethical Traveler

King doesn't seem to have a death wish, but she does enjoy **exploring the exotic** and pushing her limits ... takes us on adventures few have braved.

— Susan Alcorn, Author, *We're in the Mountains Not Over the Hill: Tales* and *Tips from Seasoned Women Backpackers*

::::::

"The Ghosts on Angel Island" provides an **insightful** look into the lives of immigrants who passed through the Angel Island Immigration Station and an excellent view of what you can learn today when you visit.

— Grant Din, Community Resources Director, Angel Island Immigration Station Foundation

::::::

Ancient Cornwall still has the power to stimulate and provoke powerful and **thoughtful writing,** and King has clearly been touched by its potency. Her story **captures the essence** of our past and present.

— Tony Farrell, poet, archaeologist, and Son of Cornwall for many generations

King **writes eloquently about loss** —loss of species, loss of ways of life. But what moved me most about *Crocodile* —besides her powerful prose—is the **heroism from everyday people** to reverse those losses and heal our planet. I'm enjoying it immensely!

— Kelly Hayes-Raitt, Author, *How to Become a Housesitter: Insider Tips from the HouseSit Diva* and the forthcoming *Living Large in Limbo: How I Found Myself Among the World's Forgotten*

::::::

Goes beyond the usual cross-cultural encounter... As humor, history and adventure weave a series of uncommon experiences, armchair travelers receive a **thoroughly engrossing** read.

— Midwest Book Review

YOUR CROCODILE HAS ARRIVED

For Jeff —
My inspiration!
Fondly,
Laurie

MORE TRUE STORIES
FROM A CURIOUS TRAVELER

YOUR CROCODILE
HAS ARRIVED

LAURIE MCANDISH KING

DESTINATION INSIGHTS

In the interest of privacy, I changed the names and identifying
details of some of the people I met or traveled with. No other
alternative facts were used, and no facts were harmed during the
writing of this book.

Photos:
Cover photo, author photo, and pages 40, 60, 160: JM Shubin
xiv: courtesy SkyWalk
12: News Ltd/Newspix
50: fouroaks/123RF
72: Creative Commons: Julia's Travels
196: Creative Commons: Veton PICQ via Wikimedia
228: Public domain via Wikimedia Commons
All other photos © 2017 Laurie McAndish King

Published by Destination Insights
www.destinationinsights.com

Cover design, interior design by JM Shubin,
Book Alchemist (www.bookalchemist.net)

CATALOGING IN PUBLICATION DATA:
*Your Crocodile has Arrived: More true stories from a curious
traveler* by Laurie McAndish King

ISBN: 978-0-9986615-1-3

First printing 2017

In celebration of oddities
and ephemera

Contents

WEIRD

The Pumpkin Eater

Stories about disappearing landscapes, ancient relics and invisible energies have always captivated me. Pickled body parts are even better. Readers often find these themes surprising, or even disturbing; several have asked why I write about such odd topics. Nature or nurture, environment or epigenetics; either way, my fascination with these peculiar forms of nature stretches back to my childhood—or earlier.

The first oddity I remember was at the Museum of Science and Industry in Chicago. We lived nearby when I was a preschooler, and Dad often took my brother, John, and me to the museum. Once inside the cool, dark building I'd run straight for my favorite exhibit, a gigantic replica of a human heart designed so visitors could step inside the ventricles and have a look around. The heart's walls pulsed fiery red and the blood vessels showed up prominently so that the inside resembled a Jack-o-Lantern, its glowing walls laced with stringy threads. The beating heart's *thrump-thrump, thrump-thrump* provided an unforgettable soundtrack.

I loved that big heart, and dubbed it the "Pumpkin Eater" for reasons any four-year-old would understand. Many years later, still fascinated by both anatomy and the thrill of walk-through exhibits, I felt right at home viewing the preserved body parts described in the story "The Cabinet of Curiosities" and crawling through the worm tunnel in "The Giant Worms of Gippsland."

There were other early influences. Every summer Mom and Dad took us on camping trips to national parks. We loaded up the four-door Rambler with a heavy-duty army-surplus tent, four sleeping bags, and a green Coleman two-burner stove. For meals, my parents packed several dozen cans of baked beans, SPAM, and powdered Tang ("the drink of the astronauts"). Then we drove off for two weeks of long-distance adventure.

After days stuck in a crowded, stuffy car (and unable to escape the odor of baked beans), we'd finally arrive and the fun would begin. John and I would tumble out of the back seat to marvel at the stinky, bubbling hot springs of Yellowstone, or the

Everglades' fearsome alligators. At Dinosaur National Monument one entire wall of the visitors' center was made of glass; behind it, real paleontologists chiseled away the rock to reveal fossilized dinosaur bones—million-year-old miracles. That was the year I became fascinated with evolution, an obsession that led, eventually, to the stories you'll find in these pages about endangered elephants, tenacious sea turtles, and flightless birds.

Mom's interests in culture and anthropology were influential, too. Once our family drove to the Tama Indian Reservation to see the annual Indian Powwow and I returned home wearing a beaded belt with the word "Iowa" spelled across the back. I kept that belt long after I'd outgrown it, as a colorful reminder of people who lived in tents and worshipped gods I'd never heard of before. The Amana Colonies in eastern Iowa, founded in 1856 by German settlers, were another opportunity to visit people whose culture and religion were markedly different from our own. Communal colonies, rain dances, beaded artifacts —of course they excited my young imagination! And no wonder I love writing—years later—about gypsies and immigrants, religious relics and almost-forgotten histories.

Ephemeral themes continue to captivate me; they

feel like part of my DNA. Maybe they were part of my parents' DNA, and their parents' as well, passed along in a twisted ribbon of mystery that stretches across generations. Or maybe the excitement of walking through the interior of the beating human heart—my "Pumpkin Eater"—was imprinted on my childhood psyche the way ducklings imprint on whatever is first offered to them as a parent figure.

Either way, these particular interests have also provided a stark reminder of the pace at which we're losing national—and international—treasures. The National Park Service predicts that, based on current trends, all the active glaciers will be gone from Glacier National Park in less than fifteen years' time. I see the same thing wherever I go: loss, from the giant earthworms of Gippsland, to Trinidad's leatherback turtles, to the few remaining kiwis in New Zealand.

Yet, I'm hopeful. I return from every trip ready to write tales that dive into the intricacies of remarkable destinations and experiences. These true accounts—of magical places, the wonders of nature, and the people who work so hard to preserve them—are stories I love and want to share. I hope you enjoy them, too.

—Laurie McAndish King

Why I Travel

*The author 630 feet above Auckland (see how tiny the cars are!),
experiencing a moment of the odd euphoria that often
accompanies questionable decisions and extreme fear.*

FEAR OF NOT FLYING

AUCKLAND, NEW ZEALAND

The trouble is, if you don't risk anything,
you risk even more.
— Erica Jong

All five toes of my right foot hang out over the edge of the Sky Tower's narrow exterior walkway, 630 feet above the city of Auckland. There is no guardrail. There is nothing at all to hold onto—nothing but thin air. I try to remember why I am here. *Did I need an adrenalin rush? Was I trying to prove something? Had I come for the view?*

The truth is, I had stopped by the iconic Sky Tower on a lark, intending to ride its glass-bottomed elevator to the top of the building, enjoy the view and a cocktail, maybe even indulge in a few small plates at Peter Gordon's award-winning Sugar Club restaurant, famous for fresh, seasonal cuisine. But curiosity got the best of me.

1

Signs in the lobby recommended the SkyWalk, promising "Life on the Edge." Posters in the elevator egged me on, assuring "An Unbeatable Rush." A promotional brochure instructed: "Report to Mission Control 15 minutes before your scheduled SkyWalk." Mission Control! It sounded so exciting—how could I resist? It also sounded suspiciously NASA-like. I wondered what the technical difference was between a sky walk and a space walk. *Well, why not find out? I thought. I'm on vacation. What is travel for if not exploration, testing boundaries, and trying something new?*

Five other tourists join me at the Sky Tower registration desk, which has the bright, understaffed feel of an airport car-rental counter. *Do I really want to participate if the company is understaffed?* There isn't time to contemplate, as I've arrived just in time for the last sky walk of the day. The other tourists are all middle-aged and do not look particularly athletic. This gives me courage. *If they can do it, I can do it.*

I don't feel that way about our guide. Her name is Sandra and of course she can do it—she's twenty-something. I remember when I was young and unafraid. Sandra has the kind of matter-of-fact attitude toward altitude that suggests she hangs out on the top of tall buildings all the time—which, apparently, she does.

"I love being high," Sandra announces. This makes me nervous. "I spend a lot of time alone on the walkway," she continues. "It's my favorite thing to do besides leading tours. The sunsets are spectacular."

Sandra talks a lot. Maybe she's nervous? Or maybe she's trying to distract us, to keep us from freaking out as we think about how high up we are, how windy it's likely to be outside and how easy it would be to lose our balance.

"I grew up in a small town on the South Island," Sandra continues. "There wasn't much to do, except hang out with my pet dog. She was a collie, but she died a few years ago. I always wanted to travel, to see the world. I applied to be a flight attendant. I really wanted that job; it was my dream job. But I didn't get it." Sandra chatters on, but is vague about the reason she was rejected for the flight attendant position. "This job turned out to be even better!" she insists.

I don't exactly trust Sandra. Why was she so vague about the reason for rejection? Perhaps she simply doesn't know. But she seems like an ideal flight attendant: competent, friendly, attractive. Maybe the airline rejected her for some psychological reason. *What if she has some sort of altitude-related personality disorder? What if she feels compelled to jump from high places? Worse yet, what if she feels compelled to push strangers off tall, windy towers? How long could a person keep a malady like that in check?*

Sandra continues her chitchat as she leads us to the staging area, which is lined with lockers. They are bright and clean. All of Auckland is bright and clean. Everything goes into the lockers. No cameras, no hats, no glasses without straps. We stash our bags and pull on the orange jumpsuits SkyWalk provides. Back home in the United States, these would have made us look like a gang of convicts. *Why jumpsuits?* I wonder. None of us is planning to jump. *And why orange?* Is it some kind of psychological ploy to make us feel incarcerated, ensuring obedient behavior?

That is probably not the reason; I, for one, am planning to do *exactly* as Sandra directs. Perhaps the color will make it easier for earth-bound viewers to see us—miniscule orange particles against Auckland's bright blue sky—as they crane their necks from below.

We step into our body harnesses, and Sandra fastidiously checks and re-checks every clasp. She doesn't talk when she is checking them; she concentrates. I'm both surprised and relieved.

But I must look worried. "You will be fine," Sandra assures me, beginning her chatter again. "SkyWalk has an impeccable safety record."

I wonder what that means, exactly. Why not just say, *No one has ever been injured or even come close,* if that is the case? I also wonder why I am just now thinking about the safety record of an operation that will, momentarily, have my very life in its hands.

As we head for the door, Sandra double-checks our carabiners. Then she invites us to follow her out onto a walkway that's *maybe* four feet wide. We trail along, reluctant. The wind is surprisingly strong up here.

Is the safety-check now complete? Should *I* be checking all the carabiners, too? Should I follow the lines of rope, at least with my eyes, until I know where every single one begins and ends? Should I personally inspect each of the cables? I know there is a principle of diminishing returns at work in this mental safety review, but I'm not sure when to stop.

From this height the traffic below is clearly visible, but it is silent. The street sounds—the engine belches and children's shouts and general cacophony of the city—all have been replaced by a quiet roar that is probably the result of my fear. The view, a spectacular 360° panorama, stretches for more than one hundred miles: southwest all the way to the Waitakere Ranges; northeast across the shimmering Hauraki Gulf to Great Barrier Island.

Rising a total of 1076 feet, Auckland's Sky Tower is the tallest freestanding structure in the southern hemisphere, and it gives northern hemisphere buildings a run for their money, too. The Statue of Liberty, by way of comparison, stands a mere 305 feet tall, and the Seattle Space Needle pushes only 605 feet into that city's cloudy skies. The Eiffel Tower tops out at 986 feet. Auckland's Sky Tower *is* a world-class high.

A long needle juts up from the top of the concrete central tower, making the edifice look like a cross between an enormous jousting lance and a steampunk spaceship. The Sky Tower glows in the afternoon light, the slanting sun turning to vanilla on its pale concrete surface. Two-thirds of the way up, concentric steel structures ring the core—these support the walkway we will use. The floor of the walkway—if one could call it a floor—is made of see-through metal grating. Below, far below, is the street.

To be clear, we *are* safe—even if it doesn't feel that way. The full-body harnesses connect us via two independent safety lines to a thick overhead cable. Nevertheless, my stomach is doing flip-flops and my breathing is shallow. My mind has turned to mush. The phrase "fear of flying" begins to run through it, recalling Erica Jong's 1973 feminist treatise on sexual liberation—or at least sexual liberties. But this is not the time for nostalgic fantasies and, anyway, fear of flying is not my problem. Fear of *not* flying is the issue at hand. Or should I say *at foot?*

Oh, yes—all five toes of my right foot hang out over the edge of the walkway. My toes are just the beginning. Sandra urges us to ever more daring feats. She is acclimating us, bit by bit, to life on the edge. "OK, now try putting the toes of *both* your feet over the edge," Sandra instructs. That is the scariest part, the toes of both feet, while we are facing outward. I can do it, but not for very long. After five excruciating seconds I slide my toes back in, one foot at a time. I think I am the bravest person in the group, because no one else does it for that long.

Sandra isn't finished with us. "Turn around so you're facing in toward the tower, and then relax and lean back," she recommends.

"You've got to be kidding!" someone squeaks from behind me.

I am not ready for this. I look down. The people are very, very small—almost too small to see. It is another universe down there; it is not my world. Up here I have the sound of Sandra's voice, clear and calm. Up here I have the cool air rushing against my face and hands. Up here I have the bulk of my jumpsuit, the tension of straps around my legs and across my chest, the knot at the top of my stomach, the metallic taste in my mouth. Up here I have my fear—and not much more.

Sandra perseveres. "Just 'sit' into your body harness and then lean back. The harness will hold you. Trust me."

At first I am certain this will be impossible, but then an odd emotion overtakes me. Suddenly I feel competitive. Now that I have proven myself by standing with my toes over the edge for a full five seconds—longer than anyone else—I feel quite courageous. And I feel the need to maintain my new position of high-altitude leadership. What if one of the others *is* able to lean back out over the city? What if someone else leans out *before I do*?

I step quickly to the outside of the walkway, turn my back to the city, inch my heels over the edge and hang them off. Then, slowly, I sit down into my harness ... straighten my legs ... and lean out.

I feel so alive, so free!

I *own* the city below. The sparkling harbor dotted with sailboats, the bright grassy parks, the condos with their rooftop swimming pools—they are all mine. Somehow the expansiveness of the view has created an expansiveness in my being. I love this life in the sky, and want to stay up here forever.

But of course, I can't. Our little group has been living on the edge for half an hour, and it's time to wrap up the expedition and return to our regular lives. I have the feeling, though, that my regular life will never be quite the same. Something in me is bigger and stronger and braver than before.

And now I understand Sandra's love of heights—a love that was previously unimaginable to me. I *get* why she thinks this the best job ever, why she hangs out here alone after work. "Sandra," I begin. "Do you know if there are any tour guide positions available here at the Sky Tower?"

Wild

An Australian farmer holding one of the Giant Gippsland Earthworms in 1979. This was a short one.

THE GIANT WORMS OF GIPPSLAND
GIPPSLAND, AUSTRALIA

A third-grade classmate of mine named Jimmy told me he would eat a live worm if I paid him twenty-five cents. None of us kids knew where he got the idea to eat an earthworm, but we pooled our nickels at lunchtime one rainy day in the spring, when the worms had come up from the ground to avoid drowning in the sodden soil. There were lots of them lying on the sidewalk, ripe for the picking.

They were soft and swollen, the color of bruises, and Jimmy chose an extra-fat one for his demonstration. It wriggled vigorously as soon as he picked it up, and Jimmy threw his head back, gulped dramatically, and swallowed the creature whole. We discussed the event for weeks, arguing over whether swallowing counted as "eating" or whether we should have required Jimmy to chew it up first. Mostly, though, we talked about what it would have felt like going down—could he feel the worm wiggling in his throat? Jimmy claimed he could.

That is what I think about when I think about earthworms. It may be that this event from long ago, and the subsequent weeks of discussion with other impressionable eight-year-olds, imprinted me with a particular fascination for the annelids. Or perhaps the simple facts of their ubiquity, their wriggling pink vulnerability, and their slight phallic aspect were enough to enchant me.

At any rate, enchant me they have, so when I was traveling through southern Australia and came across a billboard advertising the "Giant Worm Museum" of course I headed straight for the worms.

I didn't know at the time that these earthworms, *Megascolides australis*, are the largest in the world, having been reported to reach a length of more than twenty feet. I didn't know the giant worms were called *karmai* by the aboriginal people, or that the nearby village of Korumburra held an annual Karmai Festival every spring for more than thirty years, at which the worm was celebrated with a lively carnival complete with an Earthworm Queen. (Festivities climaxed when a 100-foot "worm" resembling a Chinese New Year's dragon was hoisted onto the shoulders of local children and paraded through town.)

I entered the museum, a unique "world's-first" attraction housed in a low 300-foot-long building, itself shaped like an earthworm. Inside I learned many fascinating facts about the Giant Gippsland

Earthworm (sometimes shortened to "GGE"): The creature lives underground in complex, permanent burrows—one worm per burrow—feeding on roots and other organic matter, and only rarely pokes its head out to eat plants on the surface, or to escape the occasional flood.

Remembering little Jimmy and the worms that crowded sidewalks at school when it rained, I wondered what it would be like to stand in the GGEs' territory during a heavy rain. Would the ground be covered with agitated twenty-foot worms? Would they be searching for something—a tree or a fence post or a human leg, perhaps—to slither up in order to escape the flooding?

Inside the museum I crawled through a human-sized replica of the earthworm's burrow, designed to help people empathize with the life of a worm. The tunnel was narrow and dark, distinctly lacking in right angles, and seemed to go on forever. The air smelled stale. I worried about encountering organic matter. It felt like a lonely life.

There was much more to discover at the Giant Worm Museum: Each worm has 300 to 400 body segments and is pinkish-grey, except for the head and front third of their bodies, which are purple. The GGE's average size is five to ten feet in length and about an inch in diameter. But it is almost impossible to measure the worm's actual span accurately, because it can easily stretch to more than double its resting length. "Fresh body weight" is a more reliable indicator of size; adults average around seven ounces. For comparison, that's the same weight as a cup of sugar.

The museum displayed a few old photographs of people holding the worms. The most impressive one showed three farmers standing beside each other in a field—each two arms' lengths apart from the others, and all holding one specimen that was easily fifteen feet long. They were struggling to support the GGE, which drooped precariously.

I wanted to touch one of these astounding creatures, and there they were, eight live specimens housed in giant glass tanks filled with the kind of sticky blue-gray clay the GGE prefers. One of them, with a pretty purple head, rested right up against the glass at eye level, where I could see it up close.

But the museum's live worms were not available for me to touch. The creatures are so fragile their skins "can burst as they try to escape capture, and even slight bruising may result in death." I tried to imagine the skin of a twenty-foot worm bursting—how would that happen? Would it stretch so much in its escape attempt that the skin thinned and burst in one spot?

Or would some stress-induced chemical reaction occur that made the whole creature explode? Would it all happen in an instant, or would the worm die a slow death? The museum offered no details.

I did learn that *M. australis* prefer to live under stream banks and on south- or west-facing hills and require consistently wet ground in order to move and breathe in their underground mazes. If you stomp the ground above them—or bang the ground with a spade, which is the method recommended by two earthworm scientists named Van Praagh and Hinkley in their extensive 2002 report about the natural history of *M. australis*—you will be able to hear a loud gurgling noise coming from beneath you. This is the sound made by the worms moving through their wet tunnels to escape the disturbance you have created. The museum played a recording of the sound, which is remarkably similar to the gurgling slurp made by the last few ounces of bathwater flowing out of a tub. It was on a loop, and quickly became annoying.

The GGE is listed as a threatened and protected species under the Victorian *Flora and Fauna Guarantee Act of 1988*, and the government is working to save it from extinction. I located a copy of the *National Recovery Plan for the Giant Gippsland Earthworm*, published by the Victorian Department of Sustainability and Environment, and learned still more. The report is a 31-page overview of the government's objectives and strategy for saving the GGE, including natural history, management practices, and a Recovery Action Implementation Timetable. Implementation costs were estimated at AUD $1.675 million over five years.

The report also indicated that M. *australis* is hermaphroditic, meaning it is both male and female at the same time. Even so, two individuals are required for fertilization to occur, and a pair produces one egg per year at best. Incubation takes another year, and the baby worms are an impressive eight inches long when they finally hatch. The Giant Gippsland Earthworm then requires up to five years to reach sexual maturity, all of which means the species does not naturally reproduce abundantly.

As with many of Australia's native flora and fauna, European colonization meant the decline of the GGE: Reports from early Gippsland settlers include accounts of "ploughed fields red with blood," describing the carnage wreaked upon the worms. There are photos to prove it, too—horrifying shots of muddy fields carpeted with the bloody remains of chopped up worms.

As I take this all in, it occurs to me that I'm witnessing a fleeting moment in the history of the earth: that moment when a particular—and peculiar—species teeters on the edge of extinction. These creatures will probably not make it to the next century. They live only here, in a small area of just 170 square miles in Victoria, within which they are only patchily distributed. This kind of geographic isolation means there's little opportunity for genetic exchange, but it's difficult to know, because there is no method for monitoring *M. australis* without injuring or killing individual worms.

In addition to cultivation and other soil disturbances, the GGE is threatened by drought, use of pesticides and fertilizers, and even the collection of individual worms. (Computer simulations suggest that death or removal of just three earthworms from a local population would result in the extinction of that population within fifty years.)

The captive worms weren't safe, either, as it turned out. The Giant Worm Museum was permanently closed in 2012 due to "concerns about animal welfare." I wonder what became of the worms—were they released into the wild? If so, were their captors able to find a suitable place in which to relocate them, complete with a year-round stream and blue-gray clay and a south- or west-facing hill? Were there any territorial disputes when the new worms were introduced? Were the worms able to adapt to their new environment, which was undoubtedly less hospitable than the temperature- and humidity-controlled museum tanks? Are they reproducing, and maybe even slowly evolving into worms that can survive in, say, the red clay of a north-facing hill? I'll never know.

As for my third-grade friend—well, I did hear what became of him. Jimmy grew up, went off to college, and got a Ph.D. in molecular biology. These days he teaches and conducts research at a prestigious university. I have no idea what he eats for lunch.

*Showing the wing and breast markings of a juvenile redtail
hawk after banding, weighing and measuring the bird.
Notice how securely I'm holding the legs this time.*

Hooked on Hawk Hill

THE HEADLANDS IN MARIN COUNTY, CALIFORNIA

When I flinched even the slightest bit, the red-tailed hawk tightened her vice-like grip on my right thigh. Her talon was more than an inch long. It was sturdy and had a finely pointed tip that had slipped effortlessly through my jeans and pierced my soft flesh, inducing excruciating pain. The hawk was large—her wingspan was more than four feet. I figured I needed at least four hands to free myself: one to hold the bird, whose instinct was to grasp me and fly away; one to hold her free foot, so she didn't seize me with that; and two to hold the offending foot and pull out the talon, which was curved like a huge fish hook. It was quite a predicament, and not an uncommon one among inexperienced raptor banders.

Actually, as soon as I held my first bird I was hooked—in the metaphorical sense. There is something magical about seeing a bird of prey up close, looking it in the eye, and feeling its raw power. There is something addicting about being witness to its magnificent wildness.

That's why I volunteered to be a bander with the Golden Gate Raptor Observatory (GGRO), a citizen-science organization that's been tracking birds of prey in northern California for more than thirty years. It's why I was in a small, dark bird blind on Hawk Hill, in the windswept headlands just north of San Francisco. And it's why I was stuck, immobile, with a sharp talon in my leg and searing pain on my mind.

Fortunately, I was not alone. It takes a team to catch a hawk, and I was part of a group of ten banders working in four blinds that day. My blind-mate was Buzz, an experienced bander and the GGRO's Director of Research. There's no one I'd rather be in a blind with. Buzz understands the way hawks behave. He knows how to read the wind and figure out how the birds will be flying. He can look at a hawk's plumage—the subtle variations in color, the length of the flight feathers in relation to each other, the amount of wear on the feathers' edges—and determine the bird's age. And he knows how to trap a bird and handle it safely—which, clearly, I did not.

It isn't easy to catch a hawk. The other banders and I went through an extensive training program that includes learning to set up three kinds of nets—bow nets, mist nets and dho-gazzas—because different nets work best in different weather conditions, and for catching different-sized birds. Ninteen species of raptors pass through the headlands; big red-tails and the smaller Cooper's hawks and sharp-shinned hawks are most common.

We use bow nets for the larger birds, and mist nets or dho-gazzas for the smaller ones, unless it's very windy, in which case we skip the dho-gazzas because they won't stay up if there's more than a light breeze. No matter which kind we use, catching the birds is a challenge. The altitude and direction they're flying in from, the angle of approach, the wind currents, the time of day and position of the sun—all these factors play into the trapping equation.

Getting the birds out of the nets is often challenging, too. Sometimes they dive deeply into the mesh, requiring us to snip the netting to disentangle them, which means a net-repair job, which takes time away from trapping. Other times they get a wing stuck, or bite us as we try to extricate them.

We don't hold onto the hawks for very long. Once we've untangled them from the net, our job is to perform a quick set of assessments and release the birds unharmed. The first thing we do is attach a small, numbered band—issued by the federal government—to the "ankle" of each bird we catch, so it can be identified if it's captured again, either here or somewhere else. Then we measure and weigh the birds and record data: each bird's age and sex; whether their crops are full or empty; whether they appear to have any injuries or abnormalities; and the length of their wings, tails, beaks, and talons.

Obtaining those measurements can be tricky. While some birds are relatively calm, others are spirited. American kestrels, for example, are infamous for nipping. Approximately the size of a robin, these feisty falcons peck at our fingers as we remove them from the net, focusing in particular on any hangnails they can reach. (We don't wear gloves because we need to be able to feel as well as see what we're doing, and gloves would dull our sense of touch.)

Kestrels also nip at the calipers as we adjust the moveable point and attempt to align it with the exact tip of the bird's upper mandible, so we can measure the length of the beak. They bite the little plastic ruler we slip beneath their wings to measure the distance to the tip of the longest wing feather. And who can blame them?

This poking and prodding is akin to what humans might undergo at an annual physical exam in the doctor's office. While no one would characterize it as enjoyable, it's usually only mildly annoying, and as with humans, it's important for monitoring the health of both the individual and the species. Carniverous raptors, being high up on the food chain, warn us of contaminants like DDT—and, more recently, rat poison—that have worked their way into the environment and threaten many species.

It takes hundreds of volunteer field biologists to gather all this avian data. We banders work every single day of the week during the August-to-December migration season, catching hawks during most of the daylight hours. In just over thirty years the GGRO has trapped more than 40,000 hawks, keeping meticulous records about each one. But the bird I was concerned about that day was the one gripping my thigh.

"Buzz, when you have a moment, I could use some help." I spoke softly and slowly. Buzz is not the kind of person who makes sudden movements, but I wasn't taking any chances. A sudden movement would cause certain pain.

"OK; give me a minute here." Buzz was bent over a Cooper's hawk he had just caught, measuring its wing length. He did not look up.

I decided to wait for Buzz to finish his work before explaining my predicamant. He worked quickly; it would only be a few minutes. The sound of our voices made my bird nervous, and when she felt nervous she tightened her grip. As long as the bird and I were both relaxed, and no one was moving or speaking, the pain was bearable. Once Buzz finished with his "Coop," we could focus on my red-tail.

I felt a little light-headed and needed to distract myself from the pain, so I looked more closely at the raptor in my lap. Its breast feathers were bright white; the stomach was a bit darker, with buff-colored streaks. Its back was chocolatey-brown and the tail was dark brown with thin paler bands. (This was a first-year bird; the distinctive brick-red tail feathers would not grow in until the following year.) All the feathers were in good condition, and I saw no lice or other ectoparasites; that was a good sign.

I didn't want to look directly at the hawk's eyes, thinking that might antagonize the creature. But I couldn't help myself. They were mesmerizing: fierce, bright and alert, with pale golden irises.

When I saw that Buzz was nearly finished with his Cooper's hawk, I continued. "I've been footed." *Footed* is the technical term for having a hawk's talon deeply embedded in some part of your body. It's embarassing, because it means you haven't been paying close enough attention to what you're doing. You have not properly controlled the hawk's feet. You have made a stupid mistake. The only good thing about being footed is that it hurts so much you will probably never let it happen again.

Buzz turned toward me slowly, assessing the situation. It may have taken a few seconds for him to move to my side, or maybe it took a year. It was certainly a good ten minutes before he was able to pry open the hawk's clenched foot and slide the curved talon out of my leg.

Liberated from the red-tail's grasp at last, I lay down on the rough wooden floor of the blind and closed my eyes. Buzz stepped outside and released the raptor, which I'm sure seemed unconcerned as it flew away. They always are. Often a hawk will even give a quick little shiver as it flaps away, as if to shake off the memory of a close encounter with humans.

The pain subsided quickly, and soon a deep puncture wound was all that remained of my avian adventure. That was ten years ago, and even though I was freed from that hawk's grasp, I will never be free from my fascination with these wild creatures. I sustained no further injuries, but something about these magical birds captured my imagination and pierced me to the quick. And every time I look in a hawk's eyes, I am hooked all over again.

Chaik, the one-thousand-pound brown bear I visited just outside Sitka, Alaska.

Prayer Bear
SITKA, ALASKA

Chaik, a one-thousand-pound brown bear, lumbers toward me, stops, and rises to his full height—about ten feet. He looks directly at the man standing next to me and roars.

"Do you want to feed him?" the man asks.

We are forty feet away from Chaik, which would be a far-less-than-safe distance except for the fact that the hulking bruin is securely contained in a gigantic cement pit—more than half the size of a football field. It's one of two such structures that are all that remain of an abandoned paper pulp mill just outside Sitka, Alaska. I am safely situated on the walkway at the top of the seventeen-foot-high wall that forms the perimeter of the old pulp basin that is now Chaik's home. The bear is not the one who needs protection— at least not now. But that wasn't always the case.

I am visiting the Fortress of the Bear, and its founder and executive director, Les Kinnear, is showing me around. Les has been a licensed wildlife guide for more than two decades and knows more about bear behavior and biology than anyone I've ever met.

Six-year-old Chaik and his little brother Killisnoo, who weighs a mere seven hundred pounds, came to this non-profit education and rescue center as cubs, shortly after it opened in 2007. Les got the idea for it after reading a newspaper article about the state having killed three orphaned bear cubs, who would have slowly starved to death without their mother. Shooting was—and still is—the only official protocol Alaska has for dealing with orphaned cubs, but Les thought there must be a better way.

He located two huge water settlement tanks left from an old pulp mill just outside Sitka, abandoned in 1993. With their high walls, concrete floors, and controllable drainage system, they made perfect bear enclosures. After spending several years navigating a complex and often frustrating permitting process, Les established the Fortress of the Bear. Local environmentalists protested the plan at first, but have since been satisfied that the bears here are well cared for.

"How much space does a bear need, anyway?" I ask.

Les has the data at the tip of his tongue. "International zoo standards mandate at least 4,200 square feet for two adult bears. This space houses Chaik and Killisnoo in a 35,000-square-foot enclosure—that's more than eight times as large as is required." A second enclosure that's 24,000 square feet is home to three more residents: brown bear triplets Balloo, Lucky and Toby, who arrived in 2010. They were a year and a half old at the time—not yet mature enough to survive on their own—and their mother had died from eating plastic bags she found in a garbage can.

"Because they are circular, the pulp pits provide a continuous environment. There are no unnatural corners to hem the bears in," Les says. The pits have dirt floors with small berms, low-growing vegetation, scattered branches and the occasional tree stump. They look pretty much the same as the surrounding environment, except that they also include good-sized swimming holes, a bright yellow soccer ball, and a couple of old tires the bears like to play with.

"But wouldn't they be better off in the wild?" I persist.

"All the bears here were orphaned because of human behavior, and would've been euthanized if they hadn't found a home."

It turns out that bears being orphaned because of human behavior is a common occurrence. Their mothers might be hit by cars or shot by hunters. If a hungry mother bear is hanging around too close to humans and considered a nuisance, she might be destroyed for the sake of human safety.

"Is it even possible for bears and humans to live in the same area?" I wonder.

"*Yes!*" Les is emphatic. "Bears and people can live harmoniously in the same area; they have been doing so successfully on some Alaskan islands for decades. But it doesn't work so well," he warns, "when we entice bears with outdoor barbecues and pet food, and then shoot them when they come around foraging for table scraps." The cubs left behind are lost and terrified—traumatized without their mother. Because they're so anxious, it's difficult to place them in commercial zoos.

I like the way Les answers. He may know more about bears than anyone else in the world, but he plays the information out slowly, like a fly fisherman. He never provides too much for me to absorb; in fact, he holds back a little. That just makes me more curious about the bears.

"What do they do here all day?" I ask Les.

He watches them for a few moments before answering, his face softening. I've seen this look before—it's that of a proud father. "The bears here are displayed in a way that reflects their innate behaviors—they are not bored or pacing. You can see them interacting with each other and their environment."

The bear I'm looking at now, the small male named Balloo, appears to be interacting with himself. Les is watching me watch the bear. "Is that one, um ...?" I trail off.

"Yes, he's masturbating; he's doing what boy bears do," Les says.

"What else do they do?"

"Killisnoo and Chaik search for food, explore and play with the toys we provide. They also spend a lot of time in the water; they're more closely related to polar bears than to other brown bears."

"They're related to *polar* bears?" This strikes me as odd, since the nearest polar bears are nearly 1,000 miles away.

"These are ABC bears," Les tells me, part of a genetically distinct population native to the southeast Alaskan islands of Admiralty, Baranof, and Chicagof—colloquially known as the ABC Islands. The area is known for its wilderness and wildlife, including the highest density of brown bears in the world—about one bear per 1.3 square miles.

DNA analysis suggests that the brown bear (*Ursus arctos*), a species that also includes grizzlies, was an ancestor to polar bears, which then evolved to develop specializations—such as a camouflaging white coat and teeth suited for eating seals—for inhabiting the harsh Arctic.

Killisnoo and Chaik are roughhousing, but Les assures me it's play fighting, nothing serious. They tussle in the water, wrestling and swatting at each other, splashing and growling for a few minutes. Soon they settle into what looks like comfortable companionship.

"How do you know whether they're healthy?"

"A veterinarian checks them regularly for large scars or tattered ears, which would be signs of serious fighting. He also checks their paws for cuts or other injuries, like broken nails or toes."

"Are the bears happy?" I want to know.

"Everyone asks that question, and no one really knows the answer." Les is hesitant to anthropo-morphize. "What we do know is that these bears are well fed and secure. We've eliminated the stress of finding food. There's no need for them to defend their territory, to travel through other bears' territories, or to encounter larger bears that could harm them."

And even if they can't duplicate the real life conditions under which bears hunt—killing seals, running down deer, catching mountain goats on high peaks—trainers at the Fortress of the Bear can still encourage the bears to interact with their environment and hunt for their dinner. Rather than feeding the bears on a regular schedule, trainers hide food throughout the enclosures.

"What do they eat?"

"They especially love celery and lettuce, but they don't like potatoes or onions." Once again, Les strikes me as a proud father. He knows exactly what the kids will eat. "They also enjoy grapes, apples, avocados, melon, other fruits and veggies, bread, dairy, meat, chicken, and—a special treat—live fish from the hatchery at the end of the season. Lots of their food is donated by local restaurants and grocery stores." Bears are omnivores, and will eat just about anything. That's a good thing, because Killisnoo and Chaik each require thirty to forty pounds of food every day.

Les shows me how, with hand and body movements, he has trained Chaik to stand up or lie down. "It used to be that the trainers worked the bears," he says. "But now the bears work the trainers—they will make the response that gets them food. Toby, the only female here, really likes to eat. She was the first to learn to signal for more food, by putting her paws together in front of her chest."

"Namaste?" I ask. It seems the bears use the Namaste gesture we Californians all learned in yoga class—palms together in front of our chest, a prayerful reminder of the divine spark within each of us—to ask for food. As if on cue, Toby begins signaling for more food.

Les says I can feed her if I want to. I have never fed a bear before. It seems like a risky undertaking, but Les seems to think I'll enjoy it, and leads me to a hefty metal gate that opens into the animals' enclosure. It's made of exceptionally heavy-duty steel grating, painted aqua, with a space about three inches high between the ground—which is muddy from a recent rain—and the bottom of the gate. It is through this slim slot that I am to deliver apple slices to Toby.

Toby knows what's up. She wastes no time, slipping her huge paw under the door. Her claws are gigantic. The smallest one is larger than my apple slice.

Even though the fence and gate are more than enough to keep me safe, I'm scared—so scared I almost drop the apple slice into the mud. *Does mud taste bad to Toby? Will she be mad at me if I get her apple muddy?*

Toby reaches for the apple. I'm surprised at her finesse, her agility. It's almost as though she is picking up a grain of rice with chopsticks—her touch is that delicate—and I have a new appreciation of her abilities. *Namaste*, I smile to myself. Such a reverent

38

bear. No wonder the Native Americans wore bear claw necklaces to signify not only hunting prowess but also the more subtle powers of shamanism.

Then Toby pulls the apple slice under the gate, dragging it through the mud. She is still a wild animal.

And in a flash, the food is gone.

Sama is the saddest elephant I have ever seen;
I couldn't look at her without crying.

LUCKY SAMA
PINNAWALA, SRI LANKA

Sama is the saddest elephant I have ever seen. A small adult, she has only three usable legs and leans desolately against a sturdy metal fence at the Pinnawala Elephant Orphanage in central Sri Lanka. A hundred or so tourists crowd around the dusty corral that houses Sama and three adorable baby elephants. Most of them are admiring the babies, and a few lucky visitors even get to feed the youngsters from giant baby bottles. But I am looking at Sama.

Sama's right front foot and about six inches of her lower leg were blown off when she stepped on a land mine during the Sri Lankan civil war. Although the injuries themselves have long since healed, the elephant's left front leg is severely bowed from carrying her poorly distributed weight, and her back is grotesquely twisted for the same reason. But it is Sama's eyes that affect me the most.

She gazes at me with the saddest expression I have ever seen. I am surprised to discover that an elephant can be expressive, but there she is, four feet away, looking at me with a mixture of resignation and anguish. She must be in a great deal of pain. We stare at each other for a minute or so until I can't bear it any longer and turn away. I know it sounds silly, but I don't want Sama to see me cry.

Also, I don't want her to see the pity in my gaze. I've read a lot about the emotional life of elephants, and there's no doubt among animal behaviorists that elephants exhibit empathy. They respond to each others' pain or physical problems; they assist each other and comfort each other and grieve for their dead.

I don't want the nearby humans to see me crying, either, so I move on to explore more of the twenty-five-acre Pinnawala Elephant Orphanage. It's at an old coconut plantation in the forested hills of central Sri Lanka, between the ancient royal capital in Kandy and the present capital in Colombo. Established by the Department of Wildlife Conservation in 1975 to feed, nurse and house five orphaned babies found wandering in the jungle, Pinnawala is now home to the world's largest herd of captive elephants.

Sri Lanka, the 25,000-square-mile tropical island just off India's southeast shore, was once a paradise for Asian elephants. Before the British invaded in 1815, an estimated 30,000 of the pachyderms lived on the island. But according to the Sri Lanka National

Zoo, in the 1960s, "following nearly a century of game hunting and jolly slaughter by the British colonialists," the elephant population dwindled to the point of near extinction. This tragedy prompted the Sri Lankan government to found the Pinnawala Elephant Orphanage.

British colonialists were not the only threat to elephants in Sri Lanka. Drought can be a serious problem there, so over the centuries various rulers have built tens of thousands of reservoirs, called "tanks," across the country. Elephants—especially small ones—regularly fall into the tanks and get stuck. Add to that the problems of poaching, fragmentation and loss of habitat, construction of roads and railways, and human encroachment to the forest for settlement and agriculture, and the situation looks pretty grim.

Life at the Pinnawala Elephant Orphanage, on the other hand, seems quite agreeable. As much as possible, the daily routine simulates conditions in the wild. The elephants are allowed to roam freely during the day, and have formed a herd structure with stable social interrelationships. Even though each adult requires about five hundred pounds of food each day, there's ample jackfruit, banana, coconut, tamarind, grass and other vegetation for them on the reserve. There's plenty of fresh water, too, which is a good thing, because elephants drink up to fifty gallons of water a day—about as much as a standard bathtub holds.

Bathing is a primal pachyderm pleasure, and twice a day—from ten o'clock to noon and again from two to four—*mahouts* (keepers) walk the elephants a quarter of a mile through the village of Pinnawala and down to the wide Maha Oya River, where the elephants cool off, play, or just relax. It's one of their favorite activities.

Onc of the tourists' favorite activities is watching the bathing elephants. The individual animals interact with each other, splashing and squirting, sometimes lying down in the shallow rapids, rolling and lolling and generally looking like they're having a good time.

A natural environment, good care, and freedom of movement have afforded the elephants at Pinnawala opportunities to mate, and in 1984, the first baby elephant of Pinnawela was born. Today a scientifically designed captive breeding program is in place, and some of the elephants are third-generation residents.

YouTube activists have raised concerns about the treatment of animals at Pinnawala, posting videos showing that some of the larger elephants' ankle chains have chafed or injured the animals. I didn't observe that problem when I was at Pinnawala; perhaps the publicity prompted a change.

Sama is not the only notable elephant at the orphanage. The oldest tusker here is Raja. Closing in on seventy years, he is blind in both eyes, weak, and at the end of his natural life. He is a silent monolith, not interacting with much in his environment except his *mahout*, whom Raja reaches out to touch with his trunk every minute or so. Perhaps it reassures him. Raja came to the orphanage as an adult, suffering from a gunshot wound he sustained in the wild. His tusks are huge, and part of one is missing. The *mahout* explained that the exceedingly long tusk was making it difficult for Raja to eat, so his keepers sawed it off.

If the Pinnawala Orphanage is a haven for elephants, a tiny shop in nearby Pinnawala village is a haven for tourists with a sense of humor—it sells specialty items made from elephant-dung paper: booklets, boxes, picture frames, journals.

The shop walls are adorned with hand-made posters showing various stages of the paper-making process: The dung is already ninety percent fiber when it exits the elephant. It is boiled for three days—and let me just say I'm glad I wasn't around for that demonstration!—colored with natural dyes for a week, blended for three to four hours, and spread across a small screen to dry in the sun for a day. At this stage, it's a coarse product, more like cardboard or wallpaper than stationery. It is then pressed into a much finer product, scented with cinnamon or lemongrass, and proudly packaged as elephant-dung stationery and elephant-dung note cards.

It was from another poster in this informative little shop that I learned about some of the physical differences between Asian and African elephants. African elephants are larger than Asian ones, with proportionately larger ears, which are shaped like the continent of Africa—a lucky convenience for those of us trying to remember the differences, but not blessed with the excellent memory of an elephant. Asian elephants typically have patchy orange-speckled pigmentation on their faces, trunks, or ears, which African ones do not.

While African elephants all have tusks, most Asian ones do not—only about seven percent of Asian male elephants grow them. Even more interesting, Asian pachyderms have only one "finger" at end of their trunk, while the African ones have two. And, while African elephants have the expected twenty toes, Asian elephants have only eighteen; their back feet have only four toes each.

I wanted to know more about Sama, so I did a little research after I got home. It turns out this elephant, whose name means "Peace," is known around the world. But much of the information available about her online is contradictory. Sama may have had the accident in 1996, when she was six years old. Or it happened when she was two. She may have arrived at Pinnawala in 1995, or perhaps it was in 1992 or 1984.

Information published in 2011, possibly from a 1998 research report, states that Sama "is now twelve and will suffer from considerable discomfort in the future due to changes in her spine, because of her unnatural body position, trying to balance the body weight on three legs."

Sama's situation was made worse by the fact that she was beginning to experience circulatory problems, as evidenced by changes in her pigmentation. Her keepers were also concerned about the possibility that Sama might develop psychological difficulties due to her medical condition, so they contracted with a German engineering firm to fit Sama with a prosthetic leg.

The Germans were excited about the undertaking. They set up a website for what they dubbed the "Lucky Sama Project," raised money and, in 2003, constructed a cylindrical trans-tibial (below-the-knee) prosthesis of steel and cotton, customized for Sama so that it fit perfectly.

But Sama would have none of it; she managed to remove the contraption from her leg, breaking it in the process. The next day her doctor repaired the prosthesis and tried again, but with the same results.

After a third try it was determined that Sama would have the final say with respect to the prosthesis, and that say was, *No way!*

What does the future hold for Sama and Raja? They'll live at Pinnawala for the rest of their lives. I can't imagine that either will survive much longer, but I'm glad to know they are as comfortable as possible, given their circumstances.

Some of the other rescued elephants will eventually be given to zoos. Many more will be "honored" by being presented to Buddhist temples, where they will be given starring roles in traditional religious processions. But these conditions are exploitive: The animals must be taught to behave obediently in parades, submitting to human commands and control. They must walk for miles in stultifying heat and humidity, carrying their lavish—and heavy—caparisons. They must endure drums, shouting, high-decibel fireworks, and other assaults on their sensitive hearing.

Many succumb to loneliness and depression. Elephants are intelligent, emotional creatures who have evolved to live in herds and need companionship. News reports of zoo elephants dying from loneliness have documented incidences in Japan, the Philippines, Spain, the United States, and elsewhere around the world.

As I leave Pinnawala, I ponder the future of the elephants. We are learning more and more about their emotional capacity, and some places—Pinnawala is an example—seem to have figured out how to treat them ethically. Internet interlopers don't hesitate to step in with photos, videos, and pleas for action when they see mistreatment. Circuses are closing—due in part to citizen protests about inhumane treatment of elephants—and relocating their animals to wildlife refuges. I have some hope that captive elephants' lives will continue to improve.

But I doubt that there is enough time to save the species. At the turn of the twentieth century there were an estimated 100,000 Asian elephants in the world. Today there are fewer than 40,000. Their numbers are decreasing, mostly because of habitat loss, and they are officially classified as Endangered. The question is, will we humans adapt fast enough to preserve the elephants' habitat?

The wildebeest, also known as the gnu, is surely one of God's oddest creatures—but they're pretty darned smart. Who gnu?

Who Gnu?

THE MAASAI MARA, KENYA

G stands for Gnu, whose weapons of Defence
Are long, sharp, curling horns, And Common-sense.

— Hilaire Belloc
A Moral Alphabet

I have been fascinated by the gnu from an early age, doubtless because of its prominent place—the seventh letter in—in my favorite childhood reader, *The Bad Child's Book of Beasts and More Beasts for Worse Children and a Moral Alphabet*. Originally published as three separate books in the nineteenth century, the trio were combined and reissued in 1961. I have no idea why my parents, who had a modern approach to life, thought it was appropriate for me to learn to read from a book written in the previous century with "Bad Child" and "Worse Children" in the title, but they did, and I did, and there you have it: I still own the well-worn reader, and I still feel a special affinity for that particular beast.

I had seen the gnu as a child, of course. It was on *Mutual of Omaha's Wild Kingdom*, which I waited for eagerly every Sunday morning. Watching faithfully week after week as Marlin Perkins presented his cavalcade of animals—each stranger and more wonderful than the last—I hoped that one day I'd see them in real life. The gnu, Mr. Perkins explained, is a member of the antelope family, and earned its Afrikaans nickname—wild beast, or *wildebeest*—for the frightful appearance of its oversized head and neck, shaggy beard and sharp horns.

But what the wildebeest lack in attractiveness they make up for in fortitude: Every year they lead the Great Migration in a circle that stretches over a thousand miles of African savannah. Zebra, gazelle, giraffe and many other animals join in, sometimes plodding, sometimes running, and occasionally even swimming through crocodile-infested waters, all driven to find the new grasses that sprout with seasonal rains. Stealthy predators follow in pursuit, making this is the earth's single greatest movement of land mammals.

It's an epic trek—Mother Nature at her biggest, an extravaganza that puts humans in their proper place. And the wildebeest is the star of the show. I have always wanted to witness it.

I discovered that the best way to view the migration

is actually from the air—specifically, from a hot-air balloon. It positions one close enough for a good view of the individual animals, high enough to be out of the way—this is very important, considering they're prone to stampede!—and distant enough to appreciate the majesty of two million animals on parade.

Which is why, when I visited Kenya, a balloon ride over the wildebeest migration was at the top of my to-do list, despite the fact that it required me to put my trust in a sphere of the thinnest nylon—with a big hole in the bottom—and burners that ran on the same propane fuel as my home barbecue grill. My guide for the experience would be Captain Tom, an expert on African wildlife as well as on piloting an air-driven craft with only two burners and two holes—an upper vent and a lower one—as controls.

We began in the cool of pre-dawn, when light was just beginning to tint the sky. The ground crew laid out our balloon—a gigantic bright-yellow bubble, striped with red and blue—turned on a fan and opened the blast valve, releasing a rush of blinding flame that roared from the burner and gradually filled the balloon with the heated air that would carry us skyward. Dangling beneath was a wicker gondola about the size of a five-person hot tub, with seating for ten. Despite recent advances in technology, old-fashioned wicker is still the material of choice for the basket because it's lightweight yet durable enough to withstand the inevitably bumpy landings without much damage. I climbed aboard with Captain Tom and five other guests.

At first nothing much seemed to be happening; the balloon remained low and we couldn't see any animals. I was beginning to wonder whether we were in the right place.

"Are we going to go up a little higher? I asked hopefully.

"Those small hills are blocking the breeze," Tom explained. "Things'll get easier as soon as we gain a little altitude."

As we rose, the dim morning light revealed perpetual plains and low, rolling hills covered in golden grasses. Occasional small trees dotted the savannah, giving it a playful, patterned appearance. This was the *Wild Kingdom* I had dreamed about as a child, the Africa of Beryl Markham and Isak Dinesen I had read about as a teenager, the home of the Great Migration. This was the Africa I had longed to see!

As we peered into the dawn, eager for our first look, Tom filled us in on the lives of the animals below. "The wildebeest are active both day and night; they're constantly grazing," he explained. "They calve in late January or February. Well over a quarter of a million are born in about three weeks."

I did the math. "That's five hundred babies per hour—can that be right?"

"Yes," Tom agreed. "It comes out to about that. The once-a-year glut for predators makes it so more newborn wildebeest can survive their crucial first few weeks."

That reproductive rate says a lot about the perils of being a wildebeest: Although the population of about one-and-a-half million is relatively stable, they need to replace twenty percent of the herd every year. These beasts are nothing if not tough, though. The calves learn to stand faster than any other mammal, can walk within ten minutes of their birth and can run fast enough to keep up with the adult herd when they're only a few days old.

In early July, when I visited, the migration was in full swing. "There we go," said Tom as he navigated the balloon toward still-invisible migrants. "Look over there—a dozen Thompson's gazelle." The gazelle were spooked by the roar of the balloon's burner and scattered chaotically, bounding and zigzagging beneath us like frightened rabbits.

"Wildebeest facilitate the migration of other grazers," Tom explained. The general route is shaped by the availability of food and water, and the need to avoid predators. Along the way, the wildebeest also find the grasses that are highest in phosphorous, which lactating females need. They also select the grasses with highest nitrogen content."

"How do they know which grasses are highest in minerals—can they taste the difference?" I asked, wondering what phosphorous and nitrogen taste like.

"No one knows," Tom said. "After the wildebeest have grazed, 150,000 Thomson's gazelle follow along and eat the leafy, new-growth grasses stimulated by the wildebeests' foraging. It's a complicated relationship scientists are just beginning to understand."

The gigantic herd has been estimated to produce 420 tons of dung each day, and supports the livelihoods of more than one hundred species of dung beetles.

The sun brightened and soon we could see wildebeest below, tens of thousands of them, stretching out forever, impossible to count. In some places they gathered in amorphous masses, grazing lazily, but below us they formed an endless single-file line, marching off the horizon to eternity.

We floated downward until we could hear the wildebeest calling out, high-pitched and whiny, a giant herd of snorting, bawling cattle. Sometimes they croaked like frogs. Occasionally the animals moaned in what sounded like pain or ecstasy—or perhaps relief, given their grassy, gassy diet. Drifting lower still, we got a good look at the beasts, which have comically spindly legs and manes that often sprout abruptly from their necks like unkempt Mohawk hairdos.

The tranquility was suddenly replaced with a monstrous roar and a belch of fire as our hot-air balloon descended a little too low. Over and over again Captain Tom floated us down to just above the treetops, then fired up the jets and whooshed us higher for another heart-stopping view. "I hope we'll see a lion today," he murmured, and within seconds a lone female appeared, flying through the tall grasses, too low for the wildebeest to see. She was heading straight for the long line of wildebeest, perpendicular to their trajectory as they marched across her field of vision. They were blissfully unaware, like toy ducks moving across the back wall of a carnival shooting gallery.

Wildebeest are sometimes called "the clowns of the savannah" because of their tendency to run in circles or otherwise cavort for no apparent reason.

I wasn't sure I wanted to see this part of the cycle of life up close, and was relieved when Tom observed that she wasn't hunting. "She's by herself. If she was after food, she'd be with a small group." The wildebeest must have seen her then, or heard her. They stopped walking and peered in the lion's direction. Several even ventured a few steps toward the lion with what looked like myopic curiosity.

Not a brilliant strategy, in my opinion—why didn't they keep moving? Finally deciding danger was, indeed, afoot, the wildebeest took off in a wild gallop. But they stayed in their single-file line, still moving perpendicular to the approaching lion. Why didn't they turn and run away? Why didn't they bunch together in a group? Was this the reason they had to have so many calves each year? "Do the wildebeest have any way of protecting themselves from predators?" I asked, as the lioness veered off. She was apparently just out for some exercise, and not in the mood to take on a tackle.

I later read that wildebeest use other cooperative behaviors, such as taking turns sleeping while others stand guard against a night attack. They even seem to understand the calls of other species, responding more strongly to baboons' alarm barks than to their other vocalizations.

"They can run at speeds approaching eighty kilometers an hour," Tom pointed out, "and the males can weigh five or six hundred pounds. They can inflict considerable harm, even to a lion. But their main protection comes from gathering together in large herds. That way there are plenty of eyes to watch for predators, and the young animals are protected by the older, larger ones."

Sadly, we saw just a short snippet of the great migration. Our balloon ride, unlike the journey of the wildebeest, lasted only an hour. When we came down it was with a bang. The descent was gentle but fast, and the basket bumped along on the ground, then tipped onto its side and rolled, dragging through the grass for eighty feet or so before it deposited us in a jumble of arms and legs.

No one was hurt, and we crawled out of the basket and walked a short distance to where the ground crew had prepared an elegant champagne breakfast. They'd covered a long table with a red cloth and set it with sparkling china. Chaffing dishes held hot bacon and scrambled eggs. The scents of warm cinnamon rolls and Kenyan coffee wafted through the air, and sunrise-colored fruit juices shone in the golden morning light.

My luxury balloon adventure couldn't have been a sharper contrast to the amazing survival spectacle I'd just observed. Wildebeest travel a thousand miles a year, every year, without a map. They know how to find the most nutritious grasses. They work together and in spite of fierce predators manage to survive in impressive numbers. I raised my champagne glass in a heartfelt toast to these creatures, who are certainly smarter than they first appear.

Who gnu?

This kiwi happens to be dead and stuffed, but it still appears somewhat lifelike if you squint a little. (This is not the same kiwi I saw snuffling through the woods at Zealandia.)

No Moa, No Moa;
There Ain't No Moa
WELLINGTON, NEW ZEALAND

Hunting under cover of darkness, I'm at a disadvantage: A red-lensed flashlight is my only source of illumination. Even that may be too much, as these are very shy creatures I'm after. They're nocturnal, and can see far more than I can in the dim light. I hear them rustling in the dry leaves and scurrying off to the side of the path, but I haven't seen one in the hour I've been out, scouring the night.

This expedition is a big deal for me. I'm halfway around the world—in Aotearoa—tracking down a rare bird. Aotearoa is the native Maori name for New Zealand. Its literal translation is "Land of the Long White Cloud," and the name resonates with a particular sadness I feel about the country. Or more specifically, a sadness I feel about the birds that once lived here, for theirs is a sorry story: Many have gone extinct since the arrival of humans. A giant goose, the fierce Haast's eagle, the odd-looking adzebill, and a fascinating bird called the moa—all once thrived in New Zealand but have since died out.

The bird I'm searching for has not disappeared, however. It's called a kiwi, and it is such a strange creature that I decided I must see one with my own eyes. The kiwi lives only in New Zealand and is flightless, for starters. It has no apparent wings or tail, and its speckled plumage looks like hair rather than feathers. It is also nocturnal, has a highly developed sense of smell and sports nostrils at the far end of its long, downward-curved bill—all unusual in a bird.

And then there's the egg. The kiwi lays an egg that is proportionately larger, compared with the size of the mother, than that of any other bird alive; the eggs can be up to one-quarter the weight of the female herself. This is an incredible feat; think for a moment of your own weight, and then consider birthing something that weighs one quarter that amount. Enough said.

These impressive peculiarities pushed the kiwi toward the top of my must-see list, so once I got to New Zealand, "See a Kiwi" was the first item on my itinerary.

To clarify a sometimes-confusing term, the kiwi bird—the critter I wanted to see—is a national symbol for New Zealand, which is why people from New Zealand are commonly called Kiwis. The fruit we call a kiwi is also called a Chinese gooseberry, and is native to China. It is so-named because it has been commercially grown in New Zealand, renamed as part of a marketing effort, and exported to the United States as "kiwifruit." I can't speak to the origin of Kiwi shoe polish, which was not developed in New Zealand but nevertheless features a prominent image of the kiwi bird on its packaging.

Back to that bird: There *is* a way to see the creature—rare, shy and nocturnal though it is. Ten minutes from the center of New Zealand's capital city, Wellington, sits a remarkable sanctuary called Zealandia. Its 550 wooded acres are protected from introduced predators by a state-of-the-art fence that completely encircles the preserve and even extends eighteen inches below ground level to keep out digging animals.

Security above ground is tough, too. When I visited one drizzly April afternoon I had to stop and open my daypack to confirm it contained no small freeloading fauna. Then I passed through a series of gates, each of which had to be closed before the next would open. They're serious about keeping out dogs, cats, ferrets and other non-native predators that could decimate the population.

Thus protected, some forty species of native birds and dozens of reptile species flourish here. Many are endangered, including a small population of little spotted kiwi (*Apteryx owenii*). It's been extinct on New Zealand's mainland since 1875, but a few individuals were recovered from a small island, bred in captivity and released in the sanctuary in 2000. In the wild, only one in twenty chicks survive, but here at Zealandia they do a little better.

The little spotted kiwi is the bird I'm here to find, the reason I'm traipsing through the dark, damp forest with a young Zealandia guide named Sara. Heavy clouds cover the moon tonight, and without our red flashlights I cannot even see the path at my feet.

Sara tells me more about the kiwi. "New Zealand evolved without any mammals," she begins.

"Really?" I am doubtful. The islands, about the size of California, surely could not have developed without a whole class of species. Even nearby Australia, with its crazy collection of animals like the echidna and duck-billed platypus, has mammals.

"OK; you got me. There were three species of bats. That left a large ecological niche open, so birds evolved in New Zealand much as mammals evolved in other places—right to the top of the food chain."

"So the birds became predators?"

"Yes, but what's even more interesting is that because there were no mammals to prey on them, many of the birds, including the kiwi, gradually lost the ability to fly. Without the capacity for flight, they no longer needed the lightweight bones typical of birds, and developed heavier ones. These, in turn, allowed the females to lay very large eggs."

That isn't to say it was easy. Producing a huge egg, I learned, places a lot of physical demands on the female kiwi. For the thirty days or so it takes to grow the fully developed egg, she must eat three times her normal amount of food—mostly worms and other invertebrates, a few berries, maybe even a small frog. She becomes so large that very little space is left inside for her stomach, forcing her to fast for the last several days before the egg is laid. The male incubates the egg— which seems only fair, given what the female has to go through.

Understandably, only one egg is generally laid per season. That worked out fine for a long time, as the kiwi had few predators. Then came the humans. Arriving from Polynesia less than eight hundred years ago, they quickly exploited the island's abundant large game, which consisted mostly of birds.

One of the first to go was the giant native goose (*Cnemiornis*), which stood about a meter tall and weighed nearly forty pounds. It laid giant eggs—as one would expect a giant goose to do—and giant goose eggs were doubtless a nutritious staple of the early islanders' diets. The giant goose was extinct by the early fifteenth century, barely one hundred years later.

The yard-long, tiny-winged, flightless adzebill—probably so named because its huge, heavy bill resembled an adze or an axe—lasted until the beginning of the sixteenth century. It also weighed nearly forty pounds, and would have made a good-sized meal.

The moa lasted a little longer. About a dozen species, all flightless, roamed New Zealand's forests, grasslands, and mountains. The smallest of them was the size of a turkey, but the largest—well, the largest moa was the biggest bird that ever lived. It was more than ten feet tall and weighed as much as five hundred pounds.

Some think moa were still alive at the beginning of the seventeenth century, and an actual mummified moa neck was found in Earnscleugh Cave on New Zealand's South Island in 1871. The famous "Earnscleugh Neck" moa mummy is a sixteen-inch-long slab of meat, skin and bristles which, as one wag put it, "looks for all intents and purposes like a large pork roast that was overcooked and hidden in a dry cave for two millennia." Despite that awful description, the moa has become a symbol of extinction, immortalized in a poem sung by New Zealand schoolchildren:

No moa
No moa
In old Ao-tea-roa
Can't get 'em
They've eat 'em
They're gone and there ain't no moa
      —Traditional New Zealand song

The flightless moa, unable to defend itself from humans, may have been destined for early extinction. But ironically, the unadaptive bird evolved in close association with a spectacularly adaptive species of plant. The lancewood tree (*Pseudopanax crassifolius*), which still grows in New Zealand's lowland forests, "learned" to survive alongside legions of hungry moa that could easily devour a sapling in a single sitting. The tree has evolved to change its appearance as it ages, its varying morphologies protected from birds in different ways at different times in its lifecycle.

As a seedling, the lancewood is a mottled brown color and blends into forest floor in what seems like an attempt at camouflage—it looks a lot like the leaf litter it sprouts up from, and would not have been easy for a marauding moa to spot.

Once it is too tall to hide anymore, the lancewood discontinues that approach and goes on the offensive.

Its small leaves grow to a meter in length and become weaponized: They turn into rigid, downward-pointing daggers, often with sharp barbs around the edges like the snout of a sawfish. Many also develop bright red warning spots near each barb. These vicious leaves would have been perfect for fending off a browsing bird.

I find all this adaptation quite impressive, but the lancewood has yet another trick up its sleeve. When it reaches about three meters high—which, by no coincidence, was the height of the largest moa— it changes its color and shape again. Its leaves lose their barbs and turn to point toward the sun. Atop a tall, straight trunk, they would have been beyond the reach of a hungry moa.

There are only about 70 individual kakapo —an indigenous flightless parrot— remaining in New Zealand.

These radical transformations in the lancewood's shape and color are fascinating, but it's those ancient giant birds that really captured my imagination. To my mind, the most impressive was Haast's eagle, the largest eagle the world has ever known. It had a foot three times the size of a modern-day bald eagle's, its longest talons were the size of tiger's claws, and its predatory power must have been phenomenal. This eagle would dive on its prey, such as the land-bound moa, at a speed of up to fifty miles an hour, piercing and crushing the flightless bird's neck with its mighty talons. Not surprisingly, the Haast's eagle died out along with the extinction of its most important food source. No moa, no eagle.

Learning about the extinctions of these incredible birds leaves me feeling sad. I guess any extinction is an unhappy event. It seems especially poignant, though, when the species in question is superlative: the biggest goose, the tallest bird, the mightiest eagle the world has ever known. The *only* adzebills.

The law against killing kiwi might have been enacted because of those giant eggs, a wonderfully renewable source of food. Or perhaps it was simply because of the taste of kiwi meat, which one European settler described as gamey and tough, adding, "Imagine a piece of pork boiled in an old coffin."

But there is good news. New Zealand's kiwi are still alive. This may be in part because, except for the chiefs, Maori law forbade eating kiwi. To kill one, even accidentally, was to court death.

"It isn't mating season yet," Sara says, "but we're already hearing pairs calling to each other. The male starts; his voice is higher and shriller. Then the female joins in with a harsher, croaky kind of call."

A few minutes later, we hear one. It's a male, Sara says, about twenty feet off the path, and effectively invisible to me. She catches him with her red flashlight and we watch as he wanders through the brush, moving quickly, but not overly concerned by our presence. He doesn't look like a bird—more like a roving hairball, the size of a chicken, with a long, slender beak that he pokes into the leaves on the ground.

Before I can ask what he's doing, Sara explains in a whisper, "Their nostrils are at the far end of their bills so the kiwi can sniff out underground insects and worms in the dark."

And then he's calling again, sixteen times in a row! The sound begins like an ill-tempered toddler protesting some moderate injustice, then warbles and rises to an emphatic question at the end. A lower voice joins in from a short ways away, and they finish out the call-and-response.

"Once they're bonded," Sara adds, "a male and female kiwi usually live the rest of their lives as a monogamous couple. They call out to each other at night during the mating season; that's what we're hearing tonight." We listen awhile longer, but the two kiwi have gone—snuffling off through the forest together.

"They can live up to twenty years," whispers Sara. That seems like a long time for a bird, especially given the girth of those annual eggs, but in the larger scheme of things it's only a heartbeat, the blink of an eye … the flap of an ancestral wing.

A primal peace comes over me. Yes, the kiwi may one day be extinct, but this pair—right here, right now—is not concerned with the future. They are very much involved in the moment, foraging, nesting, rustling in the undergrowth. They are very much alive. And so am I.

Leatherback turtle thinking about laying her eggs.
This is what the beach at Matura would have looked like
if I'd been there during daylight hours.

LEATHERBACK LOVE
MATURA BEACH, TRINIDAD

Matura Beach is dark tonight. I can't make out much, except the faraway glow of a highrise hotel a mile or so away, but I'm hoping to see a leatherback turtle. The females come here by the hundreds every year to lay their eggs, depositing up to 120 at a time in nests the mothers dig into the soft brown sand.

Between the wild wind and the ocean's roar, I can't hear much either. I'm glad to be with my guide, Francis, because I'm pretty sure I'll need him to lead me back to the footpath that winds through mounds of low brush and sand back to my van in the unlit parking lot behind the beach.

Matura Beach is on the eastern shore of Trinidad, the southernmost island of the West Indies, which lies just seven miles offshore from Venezuela. It's one of the best places in the world to see the leatherback turtle, *Dermochelys coriacea*. This time of year—early May—there could be fifteen to twenty turtles laying eggs on the beach each night. By the peak of the season in June, there might be as many as 300 female turtles, each digging a nest and depositing her eggs. Sometimes they accidentally dig up another nest in the process.

You'd think the turtles would know enough to spread out, but that's no longer an option because there isn't much good habitat left. These giant sea creatures—which can reach up to 1500 pounds—require dark, secluded beaches adjacent to deep water for successful nesting. They rely on light to aid their navigation, crawling in from the ocean, which sparkles dimly in the starlight, to areas of dark vegetation on the beach. There they lay their eggs in shadow, lumbering back to the lighter-looking ocean after covering the eggs with sand. The baby turtles, vulnerable to predation and poaching by hawks and other animals—as well as humans—are safe in the darkness. This is their incubator; their nursery is the deep water nearby where offshore reefs cannot injure their still-tender bodies.

At eight o'clock in the evening it's still a little early for the turtles, but Francis is not resting. Lean and full of energy, he shouts over the ocean's roar about the life of a leatherback. "People say the turtles cry, but they don't," he hollers. "They eat a lot of jellyfish—which are very salty—and their tear glands excrete the excess salt."

Francis, who has lived on the island of Trinidad all

his life, speaks in a lively and melodic pidgen. He wears a light blue polo shirt embroidered with a logo and the words *Nature Seekers Official Tour Guide,* which is helpful because I can barely see his skin in the dark. I'll have to stay close if I don't want to get lost.

"When they come outta the sand, it's like a volcano erupting. The first ones out wait for the others," he explains. This is only one of the clever survival tricks the leatherbacks employ: When they're all heading for the water at the same time, fewer are eaten by predators. Francis tells me about some of their other adaptive behaviors. "One female mates with five to seven males and stores up all the sperm. Sometimes a first-time mother will have some problems, but if she can't lay the eggs on her first try, she'll save them up and come back another night."

"What kinds of problems can she have?"

"She might not find the right spot to lay her eggs. The temperature of the sand determines the sex of the baby turtles: You got cool guys or hot chicks. Easy to remember." He's referring to the fact that the temperature of the sand they're laid in determines whether the eggs will hatch into male or female babies. "Look! There's Orion, and the Southern Cross. The stars are bright tonight."

Francis is right; the stars are getting brighter by the

minute. Soon there is enough light that I can just make out a turtle-sized shadow on the shore. At least I think it's a turtle. It's large and dark and barely moving. "There she is; she's making her way up!" he exclaims. "She is coming up from the surf. Few people see this!"

Fifteen minutes later the turtle has made her way about twenty feet up the gentle, sandy slope, but then she turns and heads back toward the ocean. Francis places himself strategically between the turtle and the shoreline, encouraging her to try again, and once more she heads across the sand. "Yes, she is a first-timer," he announces. "She doesn't know how to do it yet."

Climbing the low dunes and finding the right spot is an agonizingly slow process, and not very exciting to watch. "She is looking for the temperature of the sand," Francis explains. I'm shivering in the chilly wind, and am beginning to think about calling it quits when the leatherback finally turns to face the ocean. "She's moving the flipper; that's a good sign. You are gonna see eggs tonight. Once she's settled we'll see everything!"

Our turtle begins to dig, alternating her left and right flippers. "She is gonna start excavating. See, when she is going left and right, she has started." This, too, is a very slow process.

"How deep will she dig?" I ask, wondering how long we're going to be on the beach.

"See, she digs with her back flippers. So she's gonna dig deep. She'll dig out a lightbulb-shaped hole about two or three feet deep to deposit her eggs in. It's as deep as her flippers can go." Then Francis sees a problem. "She's digging on top of an existing nest, and the eggs that are already there are getting pushed aside."

"What will happen to the eggs from the first nest?" I wonder aloud.

"This is not good," Francis explains. "The eggs are gonna die. Bacteria will spread into the nest environment. The clutch will not hatch, but this is nature takin' its course." As though she understood him, our turtle stops digging and moves on. Finally she finds a suitable spot on the sand, digs her nest, and begins laying the eggs.

"There will be two types of eggs, fertile and non-fertile; the non-fertile ones make roomspace in the nest." Francis turns on his red-lensed flashlight and shines it on the hole she has excavated. We can see the eggs, which look like golf balls, plopping out of the turtle and falling down into the hole. Sometimes they come out one or two at a time; sometimes seven or eight come together. Some eggs are a little smaller than the others; these take up space—or "roomspace," as Francis puts it. I imagine they help regulate the temperature of the nest. "The egg is rubbery-like," Francis explains. "It never gets hard like a chicken egg."

After twenty minutes the turtle is finished, and appears to rest. "Now you can turn on your flashlight—she is still in her hypnotic state. You can touch her if you want to," Francis offers, explaining that while the leatherback is in this short-lived "hypnotic state" we can touch her without fear of bothering her or interfering with the reproductive process.

I reach down and stroke the turtle's flipper, which is surprisingly soft. But that's not my only surprise. Something about having watched this undertaking makes me feel close to the turtle, and invested in the outcome of her reproductive rite.

"How many of these eggs will hatch?" I ask, suddenly feeling protective.

"There's only a one-in-a-thousand survival rate, and they cannot be reared in captivity," Francis explains. "That's why it's so important for us to help the turtles."

A second guide joins Francis, and they measure the turtle's shell—this one is 117 centimeters, or just under four feet, from side to side. They also check for metal tags on her hind flippers, and, finding none, clamp one on each side. She was, indeed, a first-timer. The tags will identify her next year.

Francis detects some invisible sign and announces that our time is up. "She is finished now. Turn off your flashlight." We're back to watching by the meager glow of Francis's red beam.

He was right; the turtle has finished her short rest and begins to cover up the eggs by flipping sand into the hole. When it's adequately covered, she crawls back to the water.

Soon enough we'll be crawling back to our beds. I can't imagine being out here in the wind and cold night after night—even the turtles lay their eggs and then take off. I ask Francis how long he's been coming to the beach and why he keeps at it.

"I do this for future generations, and to preserve the turtles so we don't lose them," Francis explains. He clearly loves the leatherbacks. "I've been a guide at Matura Beach for more than twenty years. I even come here on my night off; I love to be here."

I nod in the darkness. And I get it: the stars shimmering over a black sea, the rush of wind and tides, the slow crawl of generations. As we head back to the parking lot, a strange feeling comes over me; I think it's leatherback love.

Weird

The remains of ancient baths in southern Spain. I couldn't take photos at the actual baños Arabes, *because there were naked people there who wouldn't have appreciated being photographed.*

CHOCOTHERAPY
SEVILLE, SPAIN

A young masseuse named Sandra had slathered my body in dark chocolate from neck to toe. The consistency of Hershey's syrup, it slid on, thin and cool, dripping into my armpits, pooling around my bellybutton, and trickling between my toes.

This wasn't what I'd expected when I journeyed to Seville, in the southern part of Spain, during the Holy Week before Easter. Religious processions, yes. *Semana Santa* celebrations, of course. Wonderful food and wine, surely. But a chocolate massage?

I'd been on the road for nearly twenty-seven hours and wanted to visit a local spa as soon as I arrived, to loosen my airline-induced knots and kinks. I was looking forward to experiencing Seville's own brand of hammam, knowing the Andalusian city had retained some of the flavor of its earlier Moorish inhabitants. A traveler has to take life as it comes, though, which is why I ended up lying flat on my back on a marble slab in a dark room, coated in cool, sticky chocolate.

The Arab baths, or *baños Arabes*, were in the Santa Cruz quarter of the city, just a short walk from my hotel. Housed in a sixteenth-century *mudéjar* palace that the brochure said "maintains the legacy of our *ancestros* who made public baths a treat for the senses," the ancient spa sounded like an ideal way to begin my stay in Seville. The brochure listed an anti-stress massage, which seemed fitting after my long trip. It also included several tempting "rituals," including a "My Perfect Skin Ritual," the geographically authentic-sounding "Al Andalus Ritual" (whatever that might be), and most promising, something called a "Four-Handed Ritual." I was all in for the four-handed treatment when I spotted something even more enticing: "Thermal Bath + Chocotherapy."

Chocotherapy!

With real chocolate? How was it possible that I'd never heard of this before? And how had I managed to live for decades without experiencing it? Chocotherapy sounded like an essential part of a life well lived; I wasted no time signing up for my session.

They couldn't get me in right away, so I took advantage of the opportunity to enjoy chocolate in the usual way and walked to a nearby "Chocolate and Churros" stand—one of many that dot the streets of Seville, sending their delicious aromas into the soft air to mingle with the scents of jasmine and orange blossoms, garlic and fried fish, and the occasional whiff of diesel. Seville is an olfactory extravaganza.

Although there were plenty of churros on display, the friendly cook made up a fresh batch especially for me, kneading the dough and frying up a tall mound of fluffy little columns of carbohydrate. I tasted a churro first. Exceptionally light and tender, it was almost like eating air—deep-fried, high-calorie air. It was not sweetened and would go perfectly with the glass of chocolate milk. But this was no ordinary glass of chocolate milk. Smooth, velvety, bittersweet, more the consistency of a thin pudding than a beverage, it was surely the love child of hot chocolate and pot de creme. And it was exactly right for churros-dipping. One taste explained why the chocolate-and-churros stands were all over the city. So dark and luscious— the stuff was addictive! These Spaniards really knew their chocolate.

And no wonder; I had read that Spain was the birthplace of modern chocolate. Modern chocolate? As compared with ... what? As compared with New World chocolate, the "food of the gods" of the Mayans and of the Aztecs who conquered them. The substance Mesoamericans labored over to create a drink with aphrodisiacal powers. The chocolate that explorer Hernán Cortés de Monroy y Pizarro, Marquis of the Valley of Oaxaca, had stockpiled and sent back to the Spanish crown more than 500 years ago.

New World chocolate was ground and mixed with chili peppers, but no sweetener was added. In fact, the word "chocolate" may have come from the Mayan word "xocolatl," which actually means "bitter water." Sixteenth-century Seville, home to Ferdinand and Isabella's court, had been Europe's gateway to the Americas, and Spain maintained control of the chocolate trade for nearly a century. It's the Old World Spanish who first thought to add sugar, a treat from the Canary Islands that transformed a spicy, bitter brew into the delicious elixir we know and love today; the irresistible confection that Americans eat twelve pounds of, per person, per year (the Swiss consume nearly twice that much); the stuff that would soon be enveloping my entire body.

I arrived at the *baños Arabes* ready for my chocotherapy experience. First came a long soak in the rooftop spa, where I relaxed in a heated pool and watched the sun sink into a pink sky, illuminating the steeples of a dozen nearby churches. Doves cooed, and the sweet scent of orange blossoms drifted up from the street. Heaven.

Next I was treated to the thermal baths: A comfortable, ninety-seven degree tepidarium, enhanced with a hydrotherapy device that bubbled so effusively it shot plumes of spray more than a foot above the surface of the water; a hot-tub-like one-hundred-and-four-degree caldarium that drained me of any lingering tension and a bracing sixty-one degree frigidarium that tightened my skin into tiny, startled goosebumps.

Each marble-tiled pool was in its own room, long and quiet, except for the burble and splash of water, and the occasional low murmur of other bathers. Masses of candles flickering through delicate cages illuminated ancient brick walls and high ceilings; the setting was unimaginably romantic.

I could easily have floated there all evening, wandering from bath to bath, soaking in the gentle waters, luxuriating in quiet candlelight. After an hour or so a spa attendant came to fetch me, though. It was time for chocotherapy.

She led me, dripping, to a dimly lit room dominated by a large marble-slab table, and indicated that I was to hoist myself up onto the slab. There was no chocolate in sight, but I knew it was nearby. I could smell it: big and dark and rich.

My masseuse entered and introduced herself. "*Hola.* I'm Sandra." She balanced a large bowl of chocolate sauce on the palm of one hand. "Please lie down."

I felt a bit like a corpse, laid out on that marble slab, or maybe like a mummy. But my skin came alive as

Sandra smoothed chocolate onto every inch, beginning at my toes and working her way slowly up to my neck. Then she went down to my toes, covering every inch again, just to be sure she hadn't missed any spots.

What exactly was it that covered my body? New World chocolate, thin and bitter? Or the chocolate of chocolate-and-churros, rich and sweet? I wanted to taste it in the worst way. Somehow that didn't seem appropriate, though. I wasn't familiar with the etiquette for a chocolate massage, so I determined to work out the best course of action in a silent conversation with myself:

"You *can't* lick it off."

"But I really want to. I want to taste it."

"Sandra is still rubbing it on; it would be an insult to her work to lick it off."

"I *have* to taste it. It's research."

"That would be unhygenic."

"I just soaked in the baths. I'm super clean."

"But you would look *so* stupid, licking yourself like a cat."

"And it would taste *so* good."

"Maybe it wouldn't. How do you know what's in it? Maybe they didn't want to waste sugar in a concoction that no one would ever taste, and it's just bitter chocolate powder and water."

No one would ever taste? All that chocolate—it seemed such a shame! Surely I was not the first person—nor would I be the last—who longed to lick the stuff. I imagined rows of naked ladies, a mahogany-colored sisterhood, covered with chocolate and sitting like cats, licking themselves clean. I liked the idea.

"It's sticky, so there has to be sugar in it," I persisted to myself. "Besides, that's why I have to taste it, to find out for sure."

"What body part would you lick?"

It was then that I realized I'd missed my chance, because Sandra began to swathe me in clear plastic wrap, beginning at my feet and quickly moving all the way up to my shoulders. I felt like a gigantic chocolate Easter bunny, neatly wrapped in cellophane and waiting for the big day—Easter Sunday, coming soon—when some lucky child would pluck me from my nest in a small plastic basket, rip through the see-through wrapping and bite off an ear.

Sandra interrupted my reverie. "I'll leave you here to relax for awhile, OK?"

My arms were trapped at my sides, and things were heating up fast, probably because of the airtight plastic wrap. It wasn't exactly a relaxing situation, but I was ready to be alone. Maybe I could lift my neck up as soon as Sandra left and reach an unwapped part of my chest with my tongue.

"OK," I said. "Thanks, Sandra."

It would not be unfair to say I was obsessed. Twenty minutes later I was still considering the possibility of licking off the chocolate when Sandra returned. Why, exactly, had I thought anything other than eating was an appropriate use of the tantalizing substance?

"So Sandra," I began. "Is all this chocolate supposed to make my skin soft?"

"*Si*," she replied. "Soft and hydrated." Sandra pronounced it *EE-dray-ted*. She unwrapped me efficiently and had expertly hosed all the chocolate off my body in a matter of seconds. It slid across my shoulders. It slipped down my back and belly and legs. I watched as it ran across the floor and circled into a drain. All that deliciousness—swirling away so quickly.

"Next is your sugar scrub."

A sugar scrub? After a chocolate massage? The brochure hadn't mentioned this, but what could be more perfect? I relaxed as Sandra scrubbed me down with granules of sugar suspended in a light oil. My skin sparkled like a sugar cookie, glinting in the candlelight.

And I had learned my lesson: This time I would take advantage of any opportunity to sneak a taste. As soon as Sandra turned her head I surreptitiously licked my shoulder ... and got an awful mouthful of argan oil and gigantic, crunchy sugar crystals. Bleeech! There was nowhere to spit it; I had to swallow.

As Sandra hosed me off once again, I contemplated my newly soft and hydrated skin. It had been cloaked in chocolate, dark and earthy, and then reborn, sparkling with light in an unusual, but not inappropriate, celebration of Easter Week. And although my confectionary escapade had come to a close, I still felt delicious.

The Dumpling Men of Taipei work at lightning speed. Here they are pinching off precise segments of dough and weighing them to confirm that each one is exactly five grams.

THE DUMPLING MEN OF TAIPEI

TAIPEI, TAIWAN

I was on a mission to hunt down *xiao long bao*—often abbreviated on menus to XLB—when I visited Taiwan recently. Rumored to be among the tastiest dishes on the island, XLB are neither elusive game nor wild plant life; they are, in fact, a much tamer quarry. They are soup dumplings. These are not ordinary dumplings floating in soup, however. They are *soup-filled* dumplings, a sort of meta-soup dumpling that's become a cult favorite on an island celebrated around the world for its cuisine. They are perfect little gems, tasty and delicate, yet tough enough to contain the steaming-hot broth inside. Or so I'd heard.

Oriental and exotic, *xiao long bao* sounded nothing like the dumplings I grew up with in Iowa. In my hometown, a *dump*-ling was a doughy blob that was unceremoniously *dumped* off a serving spoon into simmering chicken stock to cook up into a boulder-like mass of carbohydrates. As a kid, I'd heard plenty of talk among the moms about whose cinnamon roll recipe was the best or who had truly mastered the secret technique for non-curdling scalloped potatoes, but I never heard anyone comment on the flavor of someone else's dumplings. No one ever expected much of a dumpling.

So even though I wanted to sample the *xiao long bao*, I didn't have high hopes for them. I was more interested in their construction—and in the dumpling men who made them. How did these culinary contortionists manage to put the soup *inside* the dumplings? How many experiments had been performed as they developed and perfected the process? How many spectacular failures had there been along the way?

I imagined flat circles of dumpling dough, deposited into a miniature muffin tin-like contraption, first sealed on the sides—almost up to the top—then filled with soup, and finally ... well, how *would* one seal off a soup-filled dumpling? There must be another way.

Perhaps the dumpling was formed and sealed first, then *injected* with the soup. They might use a syringe filled with injectable broth ... but this theory, too, had several problems. If the syringe was a slim one, the bits of food in the soup would inevitably clog it up. Perhaps it was a huge syringe then, possibly nicked from a veterinarian who specialized in large animals. Do they even *have* large animals in Taiwan?

Still, what about the hole left by a needle of that size—the soup would surely leak right back out the hole, wouldn't it? The dumpling men couldn't pinch the hole shut without deforming the dumpling ... but these dumplings, I'd heard, were perfect. Mystified, I wanted to learn the secret method of *xiao long bao* dumpling preparation. And, as this was Taipei, I was going to need a guide.

I found an excellent one in Jerry, a handsome young Taiwanese man who knew all the best places to eat and drink in Taipei. In our week together we visited the shop where pearl tea was invented, the crystal-chandeliered restaurant that specializes in simple but-delicious beef noodle soup, and a hole-in-the-wall breakfast joint that's packed all day long and famous for what Jerry calls "oily stick sandwiches"—which were delicious.

We sampled the menu at a restaurant that used tea in each dish, and at another that used tropical fruits in every concoction. We enjoyed cool rice beer at a boisterous roadside cafe where diners joined together extemporaneously to sing traditional Taiwanese folk songs, and we tipped back world-class whiskey at the innovative Kavalan distillery. We were sampling the best Taiwan had to offer, and Jerry had saved the best of the best for last.

"Now we will go to Din Tai Fung, home of the world's best soup dumplings," he announced at the end of the week. "In 1993 the *New York Times* named it one of the world's top ten gourmet restaurants, and the only one in Asia. Since then it's expanded to more than one hundred locations worldwide; in 2010 one of them received a Michelin star."

"A Michelin star? For dumplings?" *Was that even a thing?* If so, these were going to be some hot dumplings. My curiosity was further aroused. "Can I see how they are made?"

"Yes, I'll tell you all about them," Jerry assured me. "*Xiao long bao* translates roughly as *small basket dumpling. Xiaolong* is also the name for the bamboo basket the dumplings are steam-cooked in. The name of the restaurant, Din Tai Fung, translates as *cooking pot peaceful harvest.*"

This information was undoubtedly fascinating, but I had suddenly become single-minded. "Will I be able to see the actual dumpling men?" I asked. "Can I watch them work?"

"Yes, you'll definitely see them working," Jerry laughed. We entered the bustling high-rise shopping center—where Din Tai Fung anchored the first-floor stores—and headed for the restaurant, a sleek, modern establishment. As it turned out, the dumpling men worked in a glassed-in room at the front, so yes, I could see them—and so could everyone else who walked by. They had no secrets.

Seven dumpling men stood at two work tables at Din Tai Fung, making two different batches of dumplings. The men were all tall and slim, and dressed indistinguishably in dark pants, long-sleeved white shirts, and long white aprons. They wore identical white baseball caps emblazoned with the Din Tai Fung logo in silky red embroidery thread. The hats had built-in white hairnets that covered the men's ears and curved down to meet their white shirt collars in the back.

Beneath the white baseball caps, each dumpling man wore a white paper facemask that covered his nose, mouth and chin. It was held on with white elastic bands that looped over each ear, so that all that was visible were each dumpling man's two dark eyes. Or rather, his eyes and his hands—all those beautiful long fingers flying as they cut and rolled and shaped the dough.

Despite my careful observation, I couldn't see anything that resembled a soup-filled dumpling. So I asked Jerry, again, how the dumplings were made. That's when he introduced me to Howard, the restaurant manager, who would eventually reveal the secret of the *xiao long bao*—and much more. "The flour skin weighs exactly five grams, plus or minus one tenth of one percent," Howard said. "Each is stuffed with precisely sixteen grams of filling and sealed with exactly eighteen folds."

He wasn't kidding about the "plus or minus one tenth of a percent" part: After pinching off each five-gram piece of dough, the dumpling man popped it onto a digital scale and checked to ensure that it conformed to the restaurant's exacting standards. It always did.

I watched as the dumpling men worked at lightening speed: They cut the dough into pieces; shaped and rolled each piece into a snake-like length; pinched off precise five-gram segments; weighed each one to confirm they were all exactly right; rolled them into perfectly round, skin-thin wrappers; filled the wrappers with a precise amount and pinched them closed with even, symmetrical folds. Wow—these guys were amazing!

"How long does it take to learn to make the dumplings?" I asked.

"It takes three to five years for them to learn to make the skin, pinch it off, and cut the dough—cutting the dough takes lots of practice! The chef has to pinch each dumpling eighteen times, for eighteen folds,"

Howard said. "Less than eighteen is not beautiful; makes the dumpling too soft. More than eighteen is too thick; texture too hard."

This was impressive, but I had not yet learned what, to me, seemed key. "How do they get the soup inside the dumplings?" I ventured. There were no syringes in sight.

That's when Howard let me in on Din Tai Fung's technique and the dumplings' secret. "The filling contains meat-jelly as well as meat and vegetables. It's still cool when we put it into the dumplings. When they steam, the jelly melts."

"Ah! So that's it!" I exclaimed. So simple, yet so brilliant.

"There's no secret to this," Howard assured me. "Most important is consistency, and the experience of the diner. We fill these with pork, vegetables, soy sauce. Anybody can do that."

I later learned that making perfect XLB is much more complicated than Howard let on. The dumpling skins must be made with a special kind of flour, low in protein and as fine as talc, so the dumplings are thin and pliable but do not become waterlogged. The strongest dough comes from using cold water and high-gluten flour, but a strong, stretchy dough is not the favored consistency; the chef must create a delicate balance of form and function, often using hot water first to activate the gluten and finishing with just the right proportion of cold water for a perfect dumpling skin.

Making the filling is complicated, too. The cuts of pork used must be high in fat, so the filling is the proper flavor and consistency. But if there's too much fat, there's not enough soup, which means not as much steam inside when the dumpling cooks, so the dumpling dough might not expand correctly during the cooking process. This interplay between the skin and the filling is one of the challenges of making XLBs that are both technically perfect and perfectly tasty.

Howard led us to a table and took our order. A few minutes later, when he delivered our meals, he presented the soup dumplings with quiet reverence. They were served eight to a layer in a round bamboo steam basket. The dumplings had been arranged symmetrically on a white circlet of cloth that lined the basket. The dumpling skins appeared very much like my own fingers look after too much time in the hot tub—wrinkly and translucent. Even so, those dumplings made my mouth water.

Howard stayed to be sure I ate the XLB correctly: I was to use my chopsticks to transfer the dumpling to my flat-bottomed soup spoon. "It's very hot, so you must open the window," Howard explained, showing me how to poke a "window" in the volcano-shaped skin with my chopstick. The steaming soup flowed out and into my spoon, pooling around the dumpling so it looked like a little island in a soup-spoon atoll. "Sip the soup first, then eat the dumpling," he directed.

I sipped. Still steaming, the broth was delicious: thin, yet fatty. It heated my lips, then trickled over my tongue, the aroma rising in long misty fingers. As I tipped the spoon, more broth poured from the dumpling-skin window, into the spoon and then into my mouth. It was a porcine version of Mom's chicken soup, and tasted every bit as delicious.

The dumpling itself, now somewhat deflated, was still hot, and best consumed in several bites. With any other dumpling this might have been a challenge, but because this was a perfect *xiao long bao* dumpling, expertly prepared, I had no trouble. The skin was the ideal consistency to receive my bite—firm enough to hold its contents yet delicate enough to yield to my teeth without requiring even the slightest tug or gnaw.

The savory pork-and-chive filling was in perfect proportion to the skin, and released still more rich broth when I chewed it. These were nothing like the dumplings back in Iowa. Each one was, indeed, a little gem.

My curiosity may have been satisfied, but my appetite was not. The dumplings were every bit as delicious as I had hoped. So I reached for one more *xiao long bao*. "Ah, my darling dumpling," I murmured, opening its window, lifting the spoon to my lips and breathing in the warm aroma. "Jerry was right. You are perfection itself. Or rather, you *were*." And I swallowed the last bite.

The flamenco dancer and guitarist in Seville whose fiery and passionate performances provided my first taste of duende.

FINDING MY INNER GYPSY

SEVILLE, SPAIN

When I was a little girl, I wanted to be a gypsy. Gypsies got to travel anywhere in the world. They lived in wagons that looked like fancy playhouses with big wooden wheels and bright curtains and lanterns that glowed at night. Gypsies knew how to play guitar, danced like firestorms, and could foretell the future. The women wore red dresses and sparkly gold hoop earrings. Some of them even had gold teeth!

All that I knew for certain, but there were other things I suspected. Gypsies seemed to have a special status that exempted them from having to abide by laws, which some regular adults resented, probably because they were crabby and narrow-minded from spending way too much time at office jobs. I was pretty sure gypsies didn't have to do any work, besides chopping firewood and hunting rabbits to eat. Gypsies were free.

I wanted to run away with the gypsies. I was sure they would take me; they had a reputation for that. I would *become* a gypsy, and make my living telling fortunes. We would travel the world, eating campfire food and dancing until dawn. These fantasies swirled in my eight-year-old mind as I danced on our front porch wearing my favorite skirt, the red one with three layers of ruffles, and hoping some gypsies would drive by.

As I prepared to visit Andalusia many years later—after spending way too much time, myself, at office jobs—my early gypsy fantasies returned. This time they were even more romantic: Greg Allman and Bob Dylan had sung about gypsies. So had Fleetwood Mac, Van Morrison and Bonnie Raitt.

Andalusia was the crossroads of cultures for centuries and the birthplace of flamenco, which was later adopted by gypsies. The region might give me a glimpse of the culture that had inhabited my childhood imagination and inspired my love of travel. But now my fantasies were juxtaposed with disturbing things I'd heard about gypsies in the intervening years.

A TV documentary had shown them scamming residents of Los Angeles by installing poor quality asphalt and roofing, then disappearing before their customers could complain—and before lawyers could retaliate. Gypsies apparently lied and thieved. Not only that, they also hoarded gold and married off their daughters at far too young an age. What sort of gypsy would I find in Andalusia?

I arrived during *Semana Santa*—Holy Week, the week before Easter—which turned out to be a perfect time to visit. The city of Seville was alive with preparations and celebrations by the members of *hermandads*, or religious brotherhoods, which have celebrated *Semana Santa* for centuries with processions of elaborate floats called *pasos*. My first stop was at the gypsy church, the Iglesia del Cristo de los Gitanos de Sevilla. Its brotherhood, the Real, Ilustre y Fervorosa Hermandad Sacramental, Ánimas Benditas y Cofradía de Nazarenos de Nuestro Padre Jesús de la Salud y María Santísima de las Angustias Coronada—also known as the Hermandad de los Gitanos, or Brotherhood of the Gypsies—was established in 1753.

No one at the church wore red. I saw no gold teeth, either. The people there looked just like everyone else in Seville. Some of my other preconceived notions were mistaken, too. I'd thought that perhaps a gypsy brotherhood would be poor—all that travel had to be expensive, and how much wealth can roofers and rabbit hunters amass, anyway?

But the Hermandad de los Gitanos' gorgeous *pasos* told another story. Chapel-sized exaltations of intricately worked gold and silver—some as delicate as the finest lace—they held literally tons of precious metals. How had the gypsies accumulated all this wealth? Did they steal it? I felt guilty just imagining such behavior.

In recent times, financial support came from the late María del Rosario Cayetana Alfonsa Victoria Eugenia Francisca Fitz-James-Stuart y de Silva, the 18th Duchess of Alba. The Duchess was not a gypsy herself, but she shared their free-spirited approach to life, and her tomb was in the gypsy church.

A billionaire several times over—until a few years ago, when she distributed her wealth to heirs in an attempt to placate them ahead of her marriage, at eighty-five, to a civil servant twenty-five years her junior—the Duchess held forty-nine inherited titles (a Guinness record; she was the senior illegitimate descendant of King James II of England, and the most titled aristocrat in the world).

The Duchess was inducted into *Vanity Fair's* International Best-Dressed List Hall of Fame in 2011.

The Duchess was well known throughout Europe for her eccentric habits and appearance, and was a darling of gossip magazines until her death in 2014. Her main home was a sprawling palace just a few blocks from the Hermandad de los Gitanos, and she had been quite fond of the brotherhood, providing significant gifts and financial infusions for many years.

My next stop was Triana, the gypsy quarter of

Seville and historic home to painters, potters, bullfighters and other poor-yet-noble inhabitants— including the gypsy Carmen, perhaps the most celebrated opera character of all time. Carmen still haunts Triana's twisting lanes. She enchants in the afternoon heat, strolling beneath fragrant-blossomed orange trees and their sudden, startling perfume. And she smolders as soon as darkness falls, pouting behind mysterious latticed windows and taunting all who pass. Triana is a district of artists and lovers, secrets and seduction, pain and passion.

The best place to find gypsy passion today, I decided, was in flamenco. I began at the Cristina Hoyas Flamenco Dance Museum, where I learned that flamenco was adopted by the gypsies when they arrived in Moorish Andalusia in the fifteenth century. Now it is a pastiche "of Greek methods and African drums, of Andalusian folk music and Castilian ballads ... Born in Andalusia and citizen of the world."

The museum was like flamenco itself, echoing Triana's twisting lanes and assaulting my senses with vibrant paintings, festive music and dramatic performance. The brightness was modulated by flickering historical films shown through gauzy curtains, by decaying musical instruments resurrected from some shadowy past, and by once-flaming costumes now disintegrating, slowly, to dust. I was inspired to attend a flamenco dance class at the museum. Perhaps I could at least learn the arm movements; they seemed simple enough.

As it turned out, nothing about flamenco is simple. First of all, it requires an excellent sense of rhythm, which I will never possess. Once the rhythm is established—"stomp-clap-clap-clap" is the most straightforward of many variations—one learns the walk, and then the arm movements. Next come the wrist movements (twisting from the inside out, and then the reverse) and the finger movements, and then the hip movements and the shoulder shimmy.

These seven basic movements are combined, by those who can do so, into a fiery, fast-paced dance, emotional and expressive. But for me, it was hopeless. True, I had become a traveler like the gypsies were, but I was not rich or free in the way they were. I had no hoards of gold, nor red roses between my teeth. I wondered why they'd had a hold on me all these years, and why I felt as though I somehow belonged to the gypsy tribe.

I moved from my hobbled attempts at flamenco to seeing a live performance. And then, finally, I understood—flamenco is not just music and dance. It is percussion and passion, love and longing, hunger and anger. It is all things gypsy—temptation, seduction, defiance. And it is *duende*, an intimate understanding of the part of beauty that is born of pain, a soulful state of evocation, of dark genius, of sorrow's deathly beauty.

Like the spirit of flamenco, which danced its way out of Triana and into the world, the dark truth of *duende*—that impenetrable emotion that is beyond conversation—has also traveled the globe. It was *duende*, not the gypsies themselves, that stole children away. And more than their colorful reds and golds, their music and dance, their travels around the world, it was their intimate understanding of *duende*, that part of beauty that is born of pain, which drew me to the gypsies.

The word *duende* may have originated as a contraction of phrase *dueño de casa* or *duen de casa*, meaning "possessor of a house." In Mexican folklore *duendes* are gnome-like creatures that live in the bedroom walls of young children, surreptitiously clipping their toenails, and sometimes removing entire toes.

Growing up in the Midwest in a Protestant culture, I was taught to hide my emotions. No one cared much about *feeling*, and certainly not about "negative" feelings—those were never to be aired in public, or even indulged in private. But the gypsies *got it*. More than a balance of dark and light, *duende* is a synthesis, a proof that darkness is not only legitimate, but also necessary. It is what my childhood self understood but my adult self had to re-learn.

In Seville I had discovered Carmen's legacy. It pervades the city, from spirited flamenco performances to the Callejón del Agua where Carmen used to dance, from the old tobacco factory where she worked to the bullring where she was stabbed to death by a jealous ex-lover. It stirred me a kind of passion that was far from my midwestern roots. And yet, in some mysterious way, that gypsy spirit brought me home.

Sign at the entrance to the Jamaica Inn, which was a center of Cornwall's sometimes-horrifying pirate trade.

CHEATER'S HIGH
BODMIN MOOR, ENGLAND

Lying, cheating, and stealing are wrong—my parents taught me that. They never mentioned smuggling, though. And I never thought much about that particular enterprise until I visited Cornwall, where the people have been moving contraband for more than 800 years.

Curious about this questionable activity, I decided to visit the Smugglers Museum, which is situated in the Jamaica Inn, the very building that was central to Cornish writer Daphne du Maurier's eponymous psychological thriller. High winds, haunting fog and treacherous moors provide the backdrop for her tale of smuggling, thievery, murder and terror. The whole business had struck me as horrifying when I read the book. Once there, I hoped to learn more about what they called the *free trader's* lifestyle—and the whole community's lifestyle.

En route, crossing the moor by bus, I had time to review what I knew. Cornish smuggling started in the twelfth century when locally produced tin began to be traded extensively throughout Europe for use in weaponry. Richard I levied a heavy tax on the valuable commodity, but impoverished miners could hardly afford to pay. Oppressive taxation—and thus smuggling—continued as subsequent rulers needed to fund various costly enterprises, including the One Hundred Years War, the Continental Wars, and the Napoleonic Wars.

By the late eighteenth century, the practice had swept the whole of Cornwall, as if carried by a relentless tide. Pretty much everyone participated: starving tinners, fisherman down on their luck, squires who liked their brandy, fishing boat owners making payments, gentlemen increasing their fortunes by ignoring midnight landings, retailers augmenting their incomes with under-the-counter sales, local men who were paid in drink for overnight use of their ponies— even government officials on the take. Poverty, oppressive taxes, and intractable tradition had combined to create a perfect storm.

Yet there is another aspect to smuggling, and du Maurier—who specialized in dark motives—understood it perfectly. "Desire to thwart the law is a basic human instinct ..." she wrote, "and the most honest of persons feels a tingle of pleasure if he succeeds, by some cunning means, in outwitting authority."

That tingle of pleasure is known to psychologists as "cheater's high." Getting away with something by being clever provides a sense of accomplishment—a thrill, even. It asserts the individual's authority against a rigged system. And psychologists have found that it triggers built-in neurochemical rewards. This cheater's high seems to apply to everyone—even to people who expect to feel guilty from cheating—as long as there is no obvious victim. And in a poor and overtaxed land, the taxman hardly seems a victim. In fact, he is seen as the actual *cause* of smuggling, or "free trading," which is accepted as the natural and inevitable result of overzealous taxation.

With that thought in mind, I stepped into the museum where a sign at the entrance set the tone:

Pirate, Corsair, Smuggler,
Freebooter, Contrabandist!

These are all romantic-sounding names conjuring up in the mind's eye stirring incidents from bygone times. But do not imagine for one minute that smugglers, like the swashbuckling pirates of the Spanish Main, are now just a part of history. The truth is that the smuggler is as active and daring today as he ever was in the past.

A rusty tin container labeled "Unecol Marshmallow" sat just inside the door. It had a false bottom. Using piles of puffy confectionary for smuggling struck me as implausible, and even silly. "They used *marshmallows* for smuggling?" I ventured vaguely, in the general direction of the man standing next to me.

"Mmm. They used every method available, and every man, too," he replied.

My new friend seemed to be something of an authority on smuggling, so I pressed for further details. "How many people did an average operation employ?"

"Well now, let's see." He closed his eyes and clasped his burly hands as if in prayer. "There would have been the men who kept watch from land—they tracked the position of government Preventive Men. And the spotsman, he was onboard and determined the point for landing. Beach access was best."

"How did they move the goods to shore?"

My friend opened his eyes again. "That was the lander's job; he mustered the muscle. The men had to work fast, and in the dark, so quite a few of 'em was needed. They might ha' used boats, or sometimes they just waded in if it was shallow."

I was getting a real education. "That sounds like a tough job."

"Yeah, but it's nothing like what the tubmen did. They was real athletes!"

"You said *tubmen*?"

"The tubman lugged two kegs tied together with a rope, one on his front and one on his back. He carried ninety pounds, and those kegs crushed the chest of more than one man. It was especially bad if they had to climb the cliffs—real athletes, they was. Of course they couldn't defend themselves, burdened down as they was with the kegs."

"I see—that would have been a problem."

"So that's where the batsmen come in."

"The batsmen."

"You know why they was called batsmen?"

"I'm sure you'll explain ..."

"They carried the bats."

I smiled.

"Scores of 'em was needed. They'd line up with their bats, or with hand pistols, to make a protection line for the tubmen. They didn't mind usin' their weapons, either."

"It sounds dangerous."

"It was. But the wreckers was more so. You seen the coastline around here?"

"I have. It's beautiful—very rugged."

"Very rugged is right, and we've always had lots of

shipwrecks, which don't hurt us none."

"I imagine they hurt the sailors ..."

"The sailors generally died, so it didn't bother them none, either, in the end." He paused. "You know how they died?"

I was beginning to get the picture.

"Some was drowned. The rest was killed by the wreckers."

I shot him a horrified look.

"See, the wreckers could legally claim any goods that washed t' shore. It was illegal to claim any salvage if there was survivors."

I swallowed hard. "Are you saying ...?"

"I'm saying the survivors was condemned to death, and it was the law that did it."

So it was true. Predatory "wrecking" was a sinister aspect of the trade, just as du Maurier had chillingly described it in *The Jamaica Inn*. Locals profited so much from shipwrecks that they encouraged the process, often going as far as using lanterns to lure ships ashore at night, and murdering anyone who survived the shipwreck. Smuggling was a terrible business.

I proceeded slowly through the museum, absorbing its chilling displays. It seems there was almost nothing that could not be smuggled, and the methods for doing so were varied and ingenious. The cleverest—and most distressing—technique involved transporting live animals. Exotic birds were sedated and tied in silk stockings, then pinned into the smuggler's raincoat and walked across a border.

> *The smuggler made the birds dead drunk by forcibly feeding them drops of alcohol. Their beaks were taped up to prevent them chirruping, should they come round too soon. Finches sold in Belgium for thirty pence would fetch seventy pence in Holland. A smuggler would carry anything from ten to twenty stockings at a time, with five birds to each stocking.*

I tried to picture a smuggler burdened with one hundred sedated finches, stashed into silk stockings, nonchalantly crossing the border between Belgium and Holland. The birds would press against his body. He could not sit. One wrong move, one slip, one bumbling stranger's bump, would crush them. There was a fine line between life and death. He surely experienced cheater's high. The exhibit was disturbing. Disturbing, and a little bit exciting.

Another display explained in detail how to build a

still for bootlegging—the first step in many smuggling careers. The headline was sensational:

£500 Every Week
Here is How it is Done!

Detailed instructions included a recommendation to keep the operation small to avoid arousing suspicion. I quickly calculated that £500/week is more than $40,000/year. If one doesn't pay taxes on that amount, it's the equivalent of $50,000—not bad for a small enterprise. And not a bad fit for a twenty-first-century writer looking for part-time work. I was warming to the concept and considered building my own still back at home. The construction looked easy enough. How hard can welding be? I took meticulous notes.

There were hollowed-out books and fruits, china figurines packed with opium, gunnysacks loaded with pearls, a French talcum powder canister fitted with a false bottom, and a stylish turban especially designed for smuggling hashish. A jaunty bag printed with "Export—Blue Mountain Ganja—Product of Jamaica" was displayed above a sign extolling the pleasures of that mirthful land:

Ah, that sun-blessed beautiful island, set in a
sea of azure blue, where music & laughter

delight the ears, and the sweet soft gentle tang
of marijuana smoke tantalizes the nostrils and
soothes the weary worrying brain of man with
dream thoughts of so many pleasures. Yes, in
Jamaica one can openly purchase bags full of
"the blessed weed" and walk away with it in a
carrier like this.

I felt a twinge of recognition. I may have traveled
with a very small amount of the blessed weed a time
or two myself (as I recall, visits to the in-laws were
involved). Did that make me a smuggler? My horror
became tinged with intrigue.

One exhibit recommended the hollowed-out potato,
a time-honored procedure and "still one of the best
methods for making a smuggle." This seemed almost
as laughable as the marshmallow-can stunt, and I
began to imagine myself hiding contraband in
potatoes and marshmallows. Harmless, I decided.
Completely harmless.

Nearby, an elegant high-heeled sandal seduced from
its spotlighted case. It appeared to offer no place for
concealment—at first glance. But a slender glass vial
had been secretly fitted into the heel, and "when filled
with diamond chips … produces large profits for the
smuggler and a worthwhile fee for the attractive and

disarming carrier." The sandal made smuggling seem glamorous. *I could be an attractive and disarming carrier,* I thought.

A corset caught my attention next. Along the inside of the top edge, short smudges marked the place it would have rubbed its wearer, just below the breast. Its secret pouch was easy to spot. I wondered how many carats this undergarment might conceal, and how many times it had been pressed into service. I imagined wearing the diamond-laden corset and sandals, and perhaps the stylish hashish-hiding turban as well. I could feel that cheater's high—*and I liked it.*

Leaving the museum, I found it easy enough to accept smuggling by impoverished miners forced to work in darkness, stooped over, often standing waist-deep in water. Some actually began to live under-ground rather than climbing rope ladders for hours every day in a hellish commute. The miners were besieged by accidents, flooded tunnels and disease. Despair and near-starvation were facts of life. So was smuggling. Who could object?

But the rich smuggled, too. They favored luxury items over food. French brandy was one of the top movers; tobacco, china, silk and lace were also popular. Was smuggling wrong when the well-to-do engaged in the practice? I had to ask myself: Can one activity be acceptable or not, depending on who's doing it, or when, or why? From what I could tell, Cornwall did not seem to have suffered from its history of smuggling. Perhaps the citizens had reformed?

Climbing aboard the bus, I asked the driver whether the Cornish still move contraband these days. "Of course not," he replied heartily. "That's all in the past." Then quickly, under his breath he added, "What is it yer lookin' for, lass?"

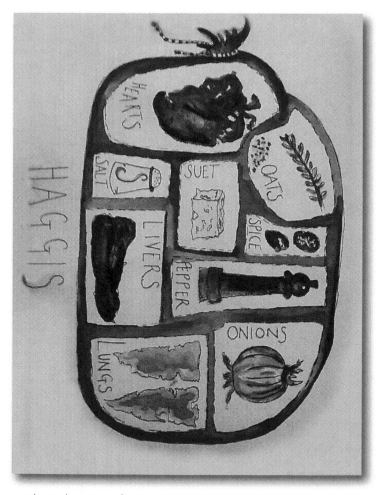

This is the piece of art we saw in the restaurant, with way too much information about the specific ingredients in haggis.

Haggis Hunter

When I mentioned my upcoming trip to Scotland, friends didn't ask whether I'd be tracking down the Loch Ness Monster or attending the Highland Games. They weren't interested in my plans for visiting world-class golf courses or drinking fine single-malt Scotches. They were not concerned, either, with windswept moors or ancient castles. They asked about the haggis.

"Eeeew—you aren't going to eat that awful stuff they make with intestines, are you?"

"It's *offal*, not *awful*," I would correct them, "and it's the national dish."

My friend Kate looked it up online. "It is a savory pudding traditionally made with oatmeal and sheep's pluck—that's the heart, liver and lungs—and cooked in the animal's stomach."

"That's disgusting." I began to worry.

"It gets even worse," Kate continued. "Haggis is often served with a classic side of bashed neeps—which is apparently Scottish for mashed turnips. That might be the actual *definition* of disgusting. I dare you to taste it."

"The Scots have been eating it since *auld lang syne*, haven't they?" I asked, doing some quick mental gymnastics. *How long* had *they been eating it? And did that really have anything to do with the way it tasted? If a whole nation had eaten something for centuries, it couldn't be too horrid, could it?* "How bad can it be?"

"So you'll taste it?" Kate asked. Her persistence was irritating.

"Of course I'll taste it; wouldn't you?"

"*I'm* not going to Scotland."

I arrived in the capital city of Edinburgh, on the southern shore of the Firth of Forth. A UNESCO World Heritage City, Edinburgh has plenty to recommend it, including the Scottish National Museum, an impressive castle, an extinct prehistoric volcano, and plenty of parks and gardens.

But I already had a plan, and had scoped out my first stop, a necessary precursor to any haggis hunt: the Whiski Rooms. In this fine establishment— recently voted Scotland's Best Whisky Bar—I could taste a flight of five single-malt whiskies, learn about their origins and eccentricities, and generally pickle myself in preparation for tasting ... the haggis. Thus fortified, I would go courageously off on my hunt. Haggis is sold at restaurants, bars, and grocery stores, so I reasoned it should be easy enough to find. In order to ensure that I didn't try to put off the inevitable, I secretly vowed to devour the very first haggis I came across—*after* my whisky-tasting session, of course.

The Whiski Rooms' decor was elegantly clubby: dark wood, low lights, sparkling glassware. A friendly bartender named Duncan made me feel at home, and I was pleased to learn they served food as well as drink. Traditional Scottish food. In fact, they served haggis.

How convenient! I'd be able to drink a flight of courage and then, without even leaving my chair, wrap my mouth around the traditional Scottish treat— subject of song and poetry—no hunting required.

Not being a whisky drinker (that was soon to change!) I asked the knowledgeable Duncan to recommend a flight. He suggested the "Introduction to Whisky Tasting" flight, which highlights regional styles and variations.

We began with a Dalwhinnie 15, a classic highlands whisky made at what is, in fact, the highest distillery in all of Scotland, which is apparently significant in some way that I do not recall. It was a pretty, pale, honey color and had a typical highlands smokiness. Duncan described it as "earthy and swampy," but it tasted mild and light to me. I liked it and downed my sample quickly.

I remember there were other whiskies. I remember thinking I'd need them, in order to face the haggis, which seemed completely unavoidable once I learned it was served on premises. Disgusting, unavoidable haggis. I remember ordering a second flight of whiskies.

I also remember discovering Laphroaig, made on the Isle of Islay. "Some people say it tastes like smoked sardines in cough medicine," Duncan said. "You'll either love it or hate it." I loved Laphroaig when I first tasted it, and I've loved it ever since. It has a butterscotch nose, but that's where the sweetness stops. On the tongue it's silky and smoky, in the mouth it's peaty, and in the throat it burns like a son-of-a-gun.

I remember my last whisky of the evening, too. I'd asked for something unique and challenging. By now Duncan and I were best friends, and he knew just what to bring me: a Mortlach 16. He described it as "chunky and oily." I adored it. The name means *Death Lake*, and it's easy to guess why. Dark and deep, complex and strong, it dragged me underwater and never let go. The stuff gave me courage, too; if I could drink a Mortlach, I could consume anything. I could even eat haggis.

And so I ordered a plate of the stuff, with bashed neeps on the side.

I'd like to report that the haggis was smooth and rich, yet surprisingly light, and offered no real indication of its offal ingredients. I'd like to report that it was deliciously savory, uniquely satisfying, my new favorite food. But that would not be true.

The truth is that I can't really remember what the haggis tasted like at all. In fact, I can't really remember much of anything after the Mortlach. But I am a woman of my word, so—although I had been temporarily waylaid by whisky—I was determined to truly taste the haggis. I would do it again. And this time I would take notes.

The opportunity arose a few days later when I visited the six-house village of Ballygown on the Isle of Mull, one of the Inner Hebrides. It's a remote area, often windy and gray, sparsely populated, accessible from the mainland only by ferry.

My husband, Jim, who was with me on the trip, managed to locate the nearest restaurant, which was closed. He also managed to convince the sous-chef, whose name was Jack, to open the place up just for us that evening even though the chef, Jack's wife, was off running an errand on the mainland. We were fortunate that Jack was able to accommodate us, because the next nearest eatery was halfway around the island, on narrow, winding roads, where all the other drivers were on the left side. In the rain, in the dark.

The restaurant was a cozy closed-in porch at the front of their house, with four small tables. I knew we were in the right place when I saw an odd piece of art hanging on the wall. It was a framed drawing that enumerated and illustrated—in full color—the ingredients in haggis: oats, heart, lungs, liver, onions, spices, salt, suet and pepper.

This sounded remarkably similar to the ingredients in a fancy French pâté I'd purchased a few weeks earlier at my local Whole Foods grocery store, which was made of pork fat, pork, pork liver, onions, spices, sherry, salt and garlic. The haggis actually sounded better than the pork fat pâté, what with oatmeal being the first ingredient, even if it was unnecessarily specific about the meat parts. I didn't really need to know which exact organs were involved.

"Do you serve haggis?" my husband asked.

"As a matter of fact, we do." Jack smiled broadly. As the sole staff in the place, he was acting as host, chef, sous-chef, server and probably dishwasher, too. "My wife makes it herself with a recipe that's been handed down for generations in her family."

"Well then, we'll take two," Jim said, with what I thought was supreme confidence. What if we didn't like it and had to leave some on the plate?

"Coming right up!"

"You know you're going to have to eat it all and maybe mine, too," I whispered to Jim. Actually, it may have been more of a hiss than a whisper. "If we don't finish it—and lick our lips—it will be an insult to this nice man, not to mention his wife and her ancestors. He's really gone out of his way to feed us tonight."

"No worries," Jim smiled. "I've got it all under control." And he poured us each a wee dram of Dalwhinnie from a small flask he had hidden in his hip pocket.

As it turned out, we didn't even need the whisky. The haggis was a small appetizer, served on big grainy crackers with homemade elderberry jam.

"You go first," I said.

"No, you go first."

"OK, let's do it together."

I brought the cracker close to my nose, delaying the moment of truth by sniffing the haggis slowly, as I would a fine whisky. There wasn't much of a smell.

When I could postpone no longer, in it went.

And it was delicious. Redolent with nutmeg, warmed by black pepper, and with a slight minerality—that was undoubtedly the sheep parts—it reminded me of a mild-flavored, perfectly textured pâté.

"What should we tell Kate it tasted like?" I wondered aloud as I devoured the last bite on my plate.

"Hmmm. We could tell her it was offal."

Here's a photo of a crocodile I shot in Costa Rica, and to me it looked the same as the crocodiles I saw in Australia—in all the important respects, anyway, like big sharp teeth and a tail that could whack you all the way from here to next Tuesday.

Your Crocodile has Arrived

THE GRAMPIANS, AUSTRALIA

In the beginning Bunjil provided us with all our needs.
He left signs by the animals to lead us to waterholes
... He continues to watch over us to ensure that we
look after the land and its resources.

—Gugidjela menu

This reminder that humans are tasked with looking after the earth, a tribute to Bunjil, the deity who created the world, is printed at the top of the menu at one of Australia's most unusual restaurants, Gugidjela. It is the first—and so far, the only—restaurant that serves a distinctively Koori aboriginal menu. Here, the traditional foods of the Koori people have been adapted with sufficient *Gugidja* (European) elements to appeal to tourists—or at least, that's the plan.

My own plan was to taste something I'd never tasted before, and I thought Gugidjela might just be the place to do it. Jim and I were visiting the

Grampians, a range of spectacular sandstone peaks in southeastern tip of Australia. According to the indigenous Australian Koori, the area, now a national park, was home to Bunjil during the Dreamtime; hence the special reverence for him. The area is still culturally important, and contains many of the continent's richest indigenous rock art sites.

Gugidjela is part of a modern park complex that includes a visitors' center with a bookstore, gift shop and interpretive displays about prehistoric crocodiles and ancient geological processes. Its menu is daunting. We consider the entrees.

"How about *Bidjin*?" Jim asks.

"No; that's fresh mussels in garlic butter," I say, reading translations from the menu. "It sounds too much like something I could get at home. Same for the *Djilga*—shrimp cocktail. I'm looking for something I've never tasted."

He tries again. "What about the *Burinj Bunjad*—smoked eel with horseradish cream?"

"No, I've eaten eel. I didn't like it at home, and I'm not going to like it here." I quickly eliminate most of the menu options. The only entrees left to consider are an emu liver pâté called *Gauwir Budjug*, which I am not sure I can stomach, and emu liver pâté with puree of bunya nuts, *Gauwir Budjug Bunya Bunya*, which doesn't sound much better.

Surely I can find something. The Koori have a wide-ranging diet. They've been feeding themselves off the land—sustainably—for a very long time, eating dozens of species of mammals, plenty of shellfish and birds, and about sixty varieties of indigenous fruits and vegetables.

In fact, theirs is one of the oldest cuisines in the world. Chef Sam Fairs, the London expat who developed the menu at Gugidjela, observed that the Kooris were eating frogs' legs 20,000 years before the French.

But if the Aboriginal foods predate French cuisine, so do their cooking methods. "Remember the kangaroo that ranger at Ayers Rock showed us last week?" Jim asks.

Indeed I do remember. The ranger had demonstrated the traditional method of cooking a kangaroo. The unskinned, uncarved, unseasoned carcass was thrown on a fire and left to char. That's it: no muss, no fuss.

"They use European cooking techniques here," I say confidently, hoping I'm right.

We bypass the appetizers and move on to the main courses. I consider the duckling, Steam-Roasted over River Sand and Bark Chips and Served with Native Pepper Leaves; the Rainbow Trout Steamed in Eucalyptus Bark; and the Grilled Baby Baramundi

Accompanied by Sweet Potato—all too similar to what I can sample at home.

What about indigenous game? The Eastern Grey Kangaroo Fillets with Wild Peach and Bush Tomato Chutney would be my first choice, but they've been crossed off the menu.

"It's apparently the most popular item," Jim says.

"Yes, I'm sure it's a delicacy, but Gugidjela is fresh out. How does Braised Saddle of Tasmanian Wallaby sound?" I reply.

"Weirdly unpalatable. Check out the next table." A waiter has just served the couple at the table next to ours.

"Your Emu Fillets," he says, placing two identical plates on the table.

"They should have hedged their bets," I observe. "What if they don't like emu fillets?" The Emu Fillets with Wild Garlic, Bush Peppers and Banksia Honey look unfortunately dark and unappetizing.

"They look like black rocks." Jim observes, before turning back to his menu. "Look—they serve Lamb in the Log," he exclaims.

Jim, who loves lamb, has found his dish. "The menu says 'swag' was a British term for stolen goods," he continues. "Traveling Australian swagmen made Lamb in the Log to avoid detection by the local squatters whose sheep they'd stolen. They seasoned the lamb and stuck it inside a hollow log hidden in the remains of a fire, where it slow-cooked in the coals."

"That actually sounds good," I say. "But I'm drawn to the *Cinga Darwinnia Citrodor*. It's pan-fried saltwater crocodile tail finished with a lemon-scented myrtle sauce."

My husband says, "I've heard that crocodile tastes like chicken."

I order it anyway. While we wait for our dinner we discuss one of our favorite Australian mealtime stories, the instructive tale of adventurers Robert Burke and William Wills. The two men set off in 1860, aiming to be the first explorers to travel all the way across Australia from south to north. Well provisioned, they hoped to achieve fame and fortune by scouting the best route for an overland telegraph line.

"They were so stupid!" says Jim. "They should win the Darwin Award." He is referring to the awards given annually to people who have done something so incredibly stupid they aren't fit to survive—or to reproduce. "They were the epitome of ignorance and arrogance."

Burke and Wills suffered a series of unfortunate incidents involving poor planning, hasty decisions, bad weather, ill health, quarrels, barely missed connections, starvation and exhaustion. The expedition ended tragically with the men badly weakened and forced to

141

survive by eating seedcakes given to them by friendly aboriginals. But Burke, who disliked depending on "inferiors" for his food, rudely refused a much-needed gift of fish, damaging the relationship. The two men starved to death soon after.

"It's too bad Burke and Wills never learned to eat witchetty grubs," Jim says, referring to the plump, finger-sized, high-protein caterpillars—larvae of the ghost moth—that have been a staple in aboriginal diets for tens of thousands of years. "The raw ones taste like almonds, but with a liquid center, and the cooked ones are crispy like french fries."

I know he's trying to gross me out. The very idea of eating a caterpillar makes me queasy, and what I've seen on YouTube—there are plenty of videos showing young white men bravely chewing the squishy, juicy critters—is positively stomach-churning.

"I'd die of starvation if witchetty grubs were a staple of my diet," I reply. "But I could eat pretty much anything else."

"That's good, because your crocodile has arrived."

The waiter sets my order in front of me. It sits, plainly plated with a light sauce and one green leaf for garnish.

It takes quite a while to cut into my first bite, and that turns out to be an important observation. The distinguishing characteristic of a crocodile tail dish—any crocodile tail dish, I am quite certain—is its unique texture. In this respect, a crocodile tail is surprisingly similar to a bicycle tire.

"You've been trying to cut that piece for five minutes."

"I know, I know; but I've got it now." I spear a small piece with my fork and lift the morsel to my lips. The lemon-scented myrtle sauce gives me hope. I bite down on the crocodile tail, only to find my teeth bouncing off it. As I regain control of my jaw I begin to realize the impact of my discovery.

After chewing for a few more minutes, I mumble, "You know what this means." I have decided to talk with my mouth full, since eating the crocodile tail is clearly going to be a full-time job. In fact, chewing it is such hard work that I now suspect crocodile tail is one of those legendary foods that require more energy to chew than they add in calories.

"What does it mean?"

"We've discovered a negative-calorie food!"

"Really? How's it taste?"

"You were right. It does taste a little bit like chicken. But only a little bit; mostly, it doesn't taste like much of anything."

"And it's apparently going to taste that way for a long, long time. Are you planning to clean your plate?"

"I can't sit here chewing all night. I wonder what

they do about people who are unable to finish their crocodile tails in one short evening."

"Well, you aren't bringing the leftovers back to our hotel room."

Jim is right. The crocodile tail will not keep well. I definitely do not want to see it again tomorrow. In fact, I don't need to see a crocodile tail dinner ever again in my life.

But there is a surprising benefit to so much chewing. I suspect that this prehistoric animal is the original mindfulness food, because it leaves me no choice but to slow down and really taste my meal. And appreciate it. The crocodile dinner has given me an opportunity to reflect on the wishes of Bunjil the Creator. Bunjil, who gave us everything we need ... Bunjil, who is still watching to ensure that we care for the land and all its resources.

Crocodile may not be my favorite dish, but as I chew, and chew, I consider gratitude. I am well nourished and healthy and grateful for the opportunity to help care for the earth and my fellow citizens. My life will never depend on my ability to swallow a witchetty grub. And, thank goodness, I didn't order the emu fillets.

Other Worlds

The remains of Tintagel Castle on the wild west coast of Cornwall, where King Arthur was conceived. Merlin's cave is off to the right, just a few minutes' hike down a cliff towards the sea.

THE MERMAID, THE CURMUDGEON, THE MAGICIAN AND THE CHURCHYARD

CORNWALL, ENGLAND

The Mermaid of Zennor was a salacious creature. Flowing hair, a sinuous body, and a bewitching voice were her most obvious attributes, but there were others. She was captivatingly beautiful. She wore no bodice—as is the custom with mermaids—sporting seaweed and pearls to great effect. And she could enchant a man with just her song. That is what happened to poor Matthew Trewhella more than six hundred years ago, at the Church of St. Senara on the wild western coast of Cornwall.

This story has been told and retold for centuries. Surely it is a myth, for mermaids do not exist—do they? Now that I have visited Cornwall, I'm not so sure. It is a remote place, magical and mysterious and home to many stories that tangle truth and legend.

The unfortunate Trewhella fellow was hardly an innocent in the affair. It was his fine tenor voice, singing praises to God in the church choir, and magnified by a particular resonance with Cornwall's cool coastal fog, that first drew the mermaid up from the depths of the sea. She began to appear in the back of the church with unnerving frequency, a long black dress disguising her pale, piscine body. Each Sunday, a small pool of water where the interloper had stood betrayed her presence.

From her position behind the last pew, the mermaid attracted young Matthew's attention.

"Your voice is so beautiful," she may have murmured.

"So you have heard me sing?" I imagine he inquired, a bit disingenuously.

"Yes, I could not resist slipping into the church to hear you sing, even though my home is in the sea and I can only venture out for very short periods of time, lest I forget how to breathe beneath the water," she likely continued—breathlessly, of course.

"And yours..." he may well have responded, enchanted by her attributes. "I imagine yours must be the voice of an angel. Tell me, are you an angel, come from the sea?"

"I am a mermaid," she surely replied. "Would you like to hear me sing?"

The two soon fell in love, the story goes, as young vocalists often do. They sang to each other from afar. Bit by bit, Matthew's church attendance declined. He frequently traipsed over to nearby Pendour Cove to search for the mermaid. And one day he disappeared.

The boy's father, understandably distraught, endeavored to outwit the lovers and secure his son's return. His plan was to play to the mermaid's conceit, employing the village woodcarver to build a beautiful chair adorned with a portrayal of the mermaid's sensual charm. (Everyone knows that mermaids are conceited; that's why they are generally portrayed with a mirror or comb in hand.) He situated the chair inside the church. Surely that would lure her back.

But it did not.

"Your father is trying to trick us," the mermaid must have observed.

"I want to be free of his controlling ways," the young man surely exclaimed. "I'm never going back again!"

And so the couple remained at their home on the rocky seabed at Pendour Cove, never again venturing onto land. The chair still sits inside St. Senara's church in Zennor, a centuries-old reminder of their love, of the sensuous dangers lurking beneath the sea, and of the mysterious power of a beautiful voice.

If the mermaid was a myth, the chair is a truth—and I wanted to see it for myself. Further, if the chair was real, then why relegate the well-known story of its origin to mythology? Perhaps the mermaid story was also true.

But the famous Mermaid Chair was impossible to view on the day I visited Zennor. The church, normally open, was locked. Tony Farrell, a local historian who was showing me around, was positively chivalrous in his attempt to get me inside. As it happened, Tony sings in the choir at St. Senara—perhaps as beautifully as Matthew Trewhella once did. Tony therefore knew that the key is sometimes kept in the nearby museum, when no one is available to tend the church, so he set off to fetch it.

But the museum was also closed, and the local volunteer who had custody of the key had just been rushed to hospital with the flu, so we had no choice but to retire to Zennor's only pub, The Tinners Arms, to refresh and regroup.

The pub sits just across a narrow gravel road from St. Senara's. Built in 1271 to serve the masons and carpenters who came to the area to construct the church, it hasn't changed much over the years. Its low, planked ceilings and cold stone floors are surely original. The ambiance inside is warm, though, and the pub's monumental open hearth is large enough to accommodate the huge bundles of crackling gorse that have tindered Cornish fires for centuries.

The Cornish ales there sounded delightful, with names like Tribute, Doom Bar, and Black Prince. But I am not a beer drinker and opted instead for a whisky, celebrating the fact that Scotland is a mere 600 miles away. The bartender, a handsome young man in a red-plaid flannel shirt, seemed unfamiliar with scotches, so Tony recommended the Lagavulin Islay for me and ordered himself a draft of St. Austell.

We sat at the very same table at which D. H. Lawrence once wrote. There were only four tables, and I spent some time at each one, just to be sure. Lawrence lived in Zennor during the Great War years of 1916 and 1917, and lodged briefly at The Tinners Arms while his cottage nearby at Higher Tregerthen was being made ready.

Higher Tregerthen, you may recall, was the home at which Lawrence's flamboyant German wife, Frieda, famously hung her red knickers out on the clothesline, provoking suspicious townspeople to assert that she was sending secret signals to German submarines off the coast, and should be forced to move from the town of Zennor. Further cause for suspicion grew from the fact that Frieda was a cousin to the infamous Red Baron, Manfred von Richthofen.

"Oh, to hell vit dem!" Frieda no doubt huffed. "I'll hang my undies vherever I please."

"It's your perfect right, Frieda!" old D. H. must have offered. "Let's go sing German folk songs at The Tinners Arms." They did.

"And bring along your boyfriend Villiam for good

measure," Frieda might have suggested. "That'll get those provincial tongues a-vagging."

"They have got the souls of insects," D. H. is known to have said, referring disparagingly to the locals. Not long afterwards and not surprisingly, the Lawrences received an expulsion order requiring them to leave Cornwall within three days.

Despite his disdain for Cornwall's living residents, Lawrence was captivated by its mysterious past. "The old race is still revealed, a race which believed in the darkness, in magic ... which is fascinating."

"It is something like King Arthur and Tristan," he wrote. "One can feel free here, for that reason—feel the world as it was in that flicker of pre-Christian Celtic civilization, when humanity was really young ...."

Lawrence was intrigued by his Celtic studies, which were fueled at the time by the early twentieth-century Celtic revivalist movement popular in Cornwall. He even tried to revive the Cornish language, making it a condition of membership in Rananim, the community he planned to found as an "anti-national protest against imperialism."

As we settled in at The Tinners Arms, enjoying our liquor and reflecting upon mermaids and Lawrence, I remembered visiting the legendary haunts of King Arthur on the previous afternoon. Camelot, which I had suspected never really existed in King Arthur's day, certainly exists now. It stands proudly on the coast of north Cornwall, in the form of the large and somewhat modern looking—for a castle—Camelot Castle Hotel, serving a luxurious cream tea to tourists along with an invitation from "Arthur" to "write a personal letter to Merlin…"

> *"He is very interested to hear about anything that you need and to hear about any wishes hopes and dreams that you have in any part of life however large or small.*
>
> *"Every letter to Merlin written at this round table will get a personal reply directly from him that you may find extremely valuable, so be sure to include your address or email on the letter and post it in Merlin's letter box …."*

Merlin's scribe was apparently not big on the use of commas.

I wrote to Merlin—who wouldn't?—and included both my email and postal addresses for his convenience. I haven't yet received a reply, but that is not a surprise. I can envision the magician in his dark cliffside cave, busily casting spells next to the furious sea. I'm sure he has lots of work to do, and doesn't have the elves, like Santa does, to assist with correspondence.

Down the hill from the Camelot Castle Hotel lies

Tintagel. Once a grand fortress, it now disintegrates on the cliffs. Wild grasses encroach on the remnants of Tintagel's stacked-stone gatehouse and wide courtyard, the placid ladies' garden and the Great Hall. Thick gray walls with regularly spaced defensive portals suggest the challenges of medieval life. And Tintagel's ancient vibes—of power and potential, danger and intrigue—are a lasting reminder of the drama of King Arthur's magical conception there.

For me, the ruins of Tintagel, barely extant, conjured ageless truths: the chivalry of the Knights of the Round Table—champions of right and good—the codes of courtliness and romantic love, and the quest for the holy grail.

My visit had made the old Camelot—in which I had not believed—much more real than the new Camelot, which I had seen with my own eyes. Cornwall was playing tricks with history.

As I sipped my whisky and mused about the tangle of truth and myth, Tony told me about the St. Senara churchyard, which I'd had plenty of time to visit while he hunted for the church key.

"Did you notice the marker, the one about Davey?"

I had seen it. The plaque on a lichen-encrusted exterior wall read:

To honour the Memory of JOHN DAVEY, of Boswednack in this Parish (b. St. Just, 1812; d.

156

Boswednack, 1891), who was the last to possess any considerable Traditional Knowledge of the Cornish Language & that of his Father & Instructor, JOHN DAVEY, of St. Just (b. Boswednack 1770; d. St. Just 1844), well known as a Mathematician & Schoolmaster, both of whom lie buried near; this Stone was set up by the St. Ives Old Cornwall Society, 1930.

"John Davey was *not* the last person to speak Cornish fluently," Tony revealed. "It was Jack Mann from Zennor—he lived at about the same time as Davey."

"He lived right here, but didn't get a plaque?" Surely the church knew about him. Zennor (current population: 271) has never been a large town.

"Jack died in 1914, but didn't receive a plaque because of his lowly status as a farm laborer."

I didn't doubt Tony's word. His family has lived in Cornwall for many generations, and his grandparents could easily have known Jack Mann.

"That's a sad story," I said.

"Yes, but it's the way the church was," he responded.

Could this be true? Had the church really ignored Jack Mann simply because of his lack of status? Would history forget him for the same reason? I wanted to know.

And I had another source. My online informant,

Wikipedia, cited Dorothy "Dolly" Pentreath, who died in December 1777, as the last Cornish speaker, even though the same article acknowledged "traditional Cornish speaker John Davey, Junior (d. 1891)" and others, including a "John Mann." So much for clearing up the confusion. The article also mentioned that Dolly was often known to curse people, frequently calling them a name she was particularly fond of: *kronnekyn hager du*—or "ugly black toad." She was said to have been a witch.

What will history remember? Online researchers will find the story about Dolly Pentreath. More rigorous scholars will discover the churchyard documentation about John Davey, Jr. And the stories about Jack Mann? Well, they may one day be lost as the locals grow old, move away, or forget.

I ordered another Lagavulin and pondered Cornwall's tangled truths.

The spectacular outermost casket in a series of seven, the smallest of which holds an incalculably valuable treasure.

THE TEMPLE OF THE TOOTH
KANDY, SRI LANKA

High above the clouds in the forested mountains of Sri Lanka sits the city of Kandy, once the capital of an ancient kingdom and now home to one incalculably precious treasure: the Sacred Tooth Relic of the Guatama Buddha. I'm not a Buddhist, but as soon as I heard about the Sacred Tooth Relic I knew I had to see it.

According to legend, mourners rescued this tooth from the remains of the funeral pyre on which the Buddha was cremated nearly 2,500 years ago. The legend doesn't specify which tooth it was—canine or molar, upper or lower—but I like to think it was a wisdom tooth. That fabled relic now rests in a golden casket, which is kept closely guarded in the eponymous Temple of the Tooth, situated at the edge of a small, serene lake in the center of the city of Kandy. The tooth attracts more than a million pilgrims each year, who come to pay their respects to the founder of one of the world's great religions. *What was it like*, I wondered, *to make a pilgrimage to a tooth?*

I had a chance to find out for myself during a visit to Sri Lanka, the teardrop-shaped island that floats off India's southeastern shore. Arab traders called the island *Serendip*, from which the eighteenth-century novelist Horace Walpole coined the word "serendipity" for his retelling of the fairy tale, *The Three Princes of Serendip*. Andrew Carnegie swore there was "no prettier sea-shore in the world" and Mark Twain said simply, "Dear me, it is beautiful!" Sri Lanka is renowned for excellent spices and tea, diamonds, rubies and other precious stones. It is said that King Solomon, who could have sent his emissaries practically anywhere in search of gems befitting the Queen of Sheba, sent them to Sri Lanka on the errand.

The Three Princes of Serendip is said to be the world's first modern mystery novel.

My hotel was located in the capital city of Colombo, more than seventy winding, mountainous miles from Kandy and the Temple of the Tooth. The concierge arranged for a local man, Shantha, to act as my driver and guide. Exceptionally handsome and six feet tall—big for a Sri Lankan—Shantha was impeccably clothed in a neat white polo shirt, dark pants, and shiny black dress shoes. His English was excellent, and he told me many stories about his country as we drove past lush tea plantations and rushing waterfalls —including tales about the fabled tooth.

"According to legend," Shantha explained, "whoever possessed the Tooth Relic was destined to rule Sri Lanka."

"Hmmm. That must have created a lot of conflict," I suggested, imagining interminable battles with legions of soldiers capturing, losing and recapturing the tiny treasure.

"Yes, my country's been in conflict for centuries," Shantha confirmed. "Our war just ended a few years ago."

"So, you grew up with it."

"It's all I ever knew."

"The people here seem quite gentle and kind," I observed. "That's surprising, given the constant conflict."

Sri Lanka's most recent warfare had nothing to do with the tooth. The extremely cruel combat, which lasted nearly thirty years, marked the birth of the world's torrent of suicide bombers.

"Seventy percent of Sri Lanka is Buddhist," Shantha replied, as though that explained everything. "About fifteen percent are Hindu and the rest are mostly Muslim and Christian." Shantha, a devout Buddhist, kept a small blue devotional book with him in the car and was happy to answer my questions about the religious practices of Sri Lankan Buddhists.

"Buddhism has five main precepts—rules we follow to lead better lives. We must refrain from killing, stealing and sexual misconduct, and from lying and intoxication. Some Buddhists practice a stricter version and adhere to additional precepts, such as abstaining from luxuries, entertainment and decoration. But it is up to each individual to decide what is best."

On the way to Kandy, Shantha continued his commentary and I was charmed by the peaceable image that emerged. Every full moon day is a holiday in Sri Lanka. Astrology plays an important role in determining auspicious days for weddings. The national sport is volleyball.

Gallup ranks Sri Lanka one of the most religious countries in the world, with 99% of its people saying religion is an important part of their daily life.

Most people use three-wheeled tuk-tuks to get around, and we shared the road with quite a few. Nearly all were embellished with bumper stickers expressing the driver's spiritual, philosophical, or political affinities:

> *Peace Begins with Smile*
> *A good driver is a better lover*
> *Tea Drinkers are Better Thinkers*
and, oddly,
> *Che Guevara!*

We dodged dogs and wound our way around cattle in the road. I watched Shantha stop to wait for a break in oncoming traffic so he could move into the other lane to avoid running over a large lizard that lay basking on the asphalt in front of us. Shantha grew visibly excited as we neared our destination, leaning forward as he drove, his voice pitched a little bit higher. He had taken hundreds of travelers to see the Temple of the Tooth, but it was still a significant trip.

We arrived at Kandy in the early afternoon. Surrounded by dense forests, lakes, rivers, and cascading waterfalls, the area is well protected from invaders and has a long history of political independence—it held off Portuguese, Dutch and British colonizers for three hundred years, until the early 1800s. Shrines sacred to the Hindu, Buddhist, Christian, and Muslim faiths have nestled in nearby hillsides for centuries.

We would visit the Temple of the Tooth the next morning, when it was least crowded. In the meantime, there was a small city to explore. Window-shopping was lots of fun, because Kandy is home to a flourishing community of artisans. Woodcarving is an especially important industry, and decorative boxes, walking sticks, toys, and souvenirs were on offer at shop after shop. My favorite motif was the fanciful *makara*, a mythical sea creature with the trunk of an elephant, the ears of a pig, the body of a fish, and—so the locals say—the aggressive behavior of a crocodile.

The ancient Kingdom of Kandy, I learned, had been an orderly domain, maintained by particularly persuasive deterrents described by a British adventurer named Robert Knox, who was detained as a "guest" of the King of Kandy in 1660. Knox spent nearly twenty years in Kandy in a loose sort of captivity and wrote extensively about what he saw. His descriptions of life there are said to have inspired parts of Daniel Defoe's novel, *Robinson Crusoe*.

Knox's descriptions included several instances of execution by elephant, in which the beasts "will run their teeth through the body and then tear it in pieces and throw it limb from limb."

The red-roofed Royal Bath House, constructed for courtly concubines, sits on the lake in front of the golden-topped Temple of the Tooth pavilion. Both were once part of a large palace complex.

Just up the street from the bathhouse sits an old theater, spacious and creaky, in which a troupe of performers dance and drum each evening in the traditional Kandyan style. Their costumes are dazzling: voluminous white sarongs, wide red waistbands and elaborately beaded red-and-gold breastplates, topped off with spectacular turbans or gold-ornamented crowns. The barefooted dancers were athletic and exuberant, but it is the drumming that was most memorable.

The three-hour performance is a masterpiece of virtuoso percussion, a persistent pulse of pounding sound, an acoustic onslaught. Riffs rise and fall, drummers slide into complex counterpoint, rhythms ebb and flow in what seems like telepathic coordination. All of it still thrummed in my head when I returned to the hotel after midnight and dozed fitfully, dreaming of elephant tusks and wisdom teeth.

It is impossible to sleep late in Kandy. A call to prayer—chanting over a loudspeaker—begins at five o'clock each morning and lasts nearly an hour. Traffic commences around six. What sounded like a thousand dogs started barking at sunrise, shortly before seven. The local birds began their cacophonous chorus a few minutes later, and at seven o'clock sharp a gong clanged three times.

After a breakfast of rice and fish curry, Shantha and I joined a throng of people moving slowly toward the Temple of the Tooth, participating in the *puja* that occurs three times a day, every day of the year. More than a thousand people waited with us in a long, quiet line—calmly, patiently, graciously—anticipating a glimpse of the Sacred Tooth Relic.

We crossed a bridge over a wide water-filled moat, passed through formidable fortress walls and into elaborate pavilions decorated with sacred texts and intricate ivory carvings with images of fanciful animals: dogs with wings, lions with human-like arms and legs. We squeezed into a narrow corridor steeped in the sweet, heady fragrances of jasmine and frangipani. In a two-story chamber, ornate panels—crowded with golden gods and goddesses, writhing green dragons and crocodiles in roiling blue seas—stretched to the ceiling. Drums beat maniacally and incense clouded the room.

Snaking past a set of glittering doors flanked by four magnificent six-foot elephant tusks resplendent in golden standards, we found ourselves deep inside the chambers that housed the golden, crown-like reliquary we had all come to see.

I'm still not sure exactly how it was that Shantha got me to the front of the crowded hall. Tall and regal in bearing, but without a trace of arrogance, he simply walked through the throng, up a staircase and across a teeming hall to the front of the viewing area. The crowds opened up and made way for us as though he were some sort of prince. I watched our wake closely and noticed that no one looked the least bit perturbed about moving aside for us; it was almost as though we were one huge organism, our common protoplasm matter-of-factly rearranging itself as Shantha and I moved to the front of the room.

No one among the thousand or more visitors would be allowed more than a glance, but Shantha showed me exactly where to stand for the best view. I would not see the actual tooth; only the first reliquary, or casket, which remained closed. Inside it sat another, and inside that sat more—a total of seven ornate boxes nested inside one another like Russian matryoshka dolls. The last one held the Buddha's tooth, far too precious to be displayed to the public three times a day. We waited.

When the interior temple doors finally yawned open, an irresistible press of bodies welled up and carried me past the reliquary in a second, but my quick glimpse was unforgettable: It stood as tall as a person and was shaped like a pope's hat, with an elaborate finial at the top that pointed to the heavens like some kind of sparkling space needle. Rimmed with golden bands, encrusted with golden medallions, dripping with ropes of shimmering pearls, it was the most magnificent creation I had ever seen. A luminous glow rippled from it, and my heart caught for a moment, thrilled. I actually thought I might be having some sort of unfortunate cardiac event, but my pulse quickly returned to normal as I was enveloped in the sweet-scented altar flowers, the hypnotic drumming and swirling incense, the elaborate decoration and vivid colors, the press of a thousand pilgrims. Now all of our hearts seemed to beat as one.

And so my first lesson in Buddhism came to a close—and it seemed subtly serendipitous. I had come to see a sacred relic, but ended up experiencing something far more precious. The reliquary that holds the Sacred Tooth Relic of the Guatama Buddha, dazzling as it is, cannot compare with the memory of one thousand Buddhist hearts beating in unison—and my own very excited Western heart beating right along with them.

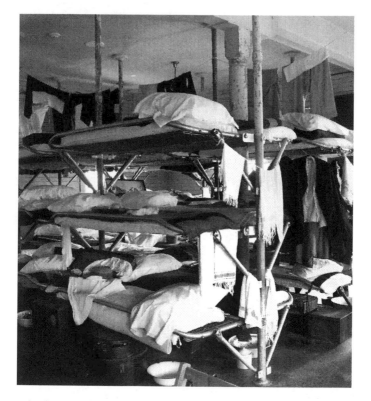

This historical re-creation shows the crowded conditions in the men's dormitory at the Angel Island Immigration Station. Chinese men were not given mattresses to sleep on.

The Ghosts on Angel Island

San Francisco, California

.... Just leave them in the shadow like a ghost town,
a ghost nation.
— Isabelle Allende

I had hiked to the top of Mt. Livermore, situated on Angel Island in the San Francisco Bay, for one of the world's most impressive three-hundred-sixty-degree panoramas. The easy path up circled the mountain, rewarding me with cool breezes, the scent of bay and eucalyptus, and alternating views of the San Francisco skyline, Alcatraz Island, the Golden Gate Bridge, the Pacific Ocean, the rugged Marin County headlands, the Oakland hills and the sparkling San Francisco Bay. It was gorgeous.

But there's another view from the island—a historical view—that impressed me even more. As I walked back down the hill towards the old Angel Island Immigration Station, the first thing I saw was the tall barbed-wire fence that surrounds the

173

compound. The gun towers that guarded its perimeter are still there, too. Imposing as the compound is now, it must have been even more so when the towers were manned day and night. Imposing and ironic: Immigrants to the Land of the Free were detained here against their will.

Inside the barbed wire are several barracks, with historical recreations of immigrants' living quarters including a men's game room that houses a ping-pong table, a record player and mahjong tiles. Visitors can also see a hospital, an administration building and the three dining halls—for Asians, Europeans, and Immigration Station staff.

I learned more from Joe Chan, who has been a docent at the Angel Island Immigration Station for more than twenty years. "My parents both entered the United States at Angel Island before I was born," Joe says, "and I grew up hearing their stories." The first-generation American has since become an expert in the history of the Angel Island Immigration Station, and shares the story of his family—and that of hundreds of thousands of other families—with visitors from around the world.

The ghosts of those families still haunt the island. There isn't much left of the long loading dock that once extended out into San Francisco Bay, but it's easy to imagine the crowds of hopeful immigrants arriving by ship, grateful, after their long voyages, to be at the easy end of an arduous journey. Or so they thought.

But the immigrants needed to be "processed" before they were admitted to their new home, and the Angel Island Immigration Station—also called "The Guardian of the Western Gate"—served as a holding station during that time. For many Asian travelers, processing was a frightening ordeal. Families were separated—men in one section, women and children in another. The rooms were locked and guarded at night. The island was considered an ideal location because it was easy to guard and even if detainees escaped, they weren't likely to get far.

Alcatraz, that other fortress of an island, is only a few miles from Angel Island.

We stand between the old barracks and the sea—Joe, myself, and three young Asian tourists. The bright blue sky and the dun-colored dust probably look just the same as they did when Joe's parents were here, more than half a century ago. But today there is something new on the spot—something Joe's parents never saw. It's a commemorative monument with row upon row of Certificates of Identity, reproduced as delicate photo-etchings on polished black marble. A little larger than a drivers license, each one shows a name, photo, birthdate, height, occupation, signature, "physical marks and peculiarities" and other identifying information about a particular immigrant.

"This is my mother's Certificate of Identity," Joe says quietly, pointing to one of the images. The three Asian girls gasp in unison. This is apparently not something they expected to see in America.

Then Joe points to a Certificate of Identity on the other side of the monument. "And this is my father's Certificate of Identity," he continues. The girls gasp again. Something about the fact that it is Joe himself, standing here, showing us his own parents' Certificates of Identity, is unbearably poignant. Everything we are about to learn about how life had been at the Immigration Station is just one generation away from the man standing next to us. It's almost as if we could reach out and touch history.

Known as the Ellis Island of the West, the Angel Island Immigration Station processed nearly a million immigrants from eighty-two countries between 1910 and 1940. But their treatment was in sharp contrast to the immigrant experience implied by the famous poem that is synonymous with Ellis Island:

... Give me your tired, your poor,
Your huddled masses yearning to breathe free,
The wretched refuse of your teeming shore.
Send these, the homeless, tempest-tost to me...

The conditions here were worse than crowded. At one time the Asian men's barracks, designed to accommodate 56 people, housed more than 200. Inside the barracks, narrow metal bunks were stacked three high, with suitcases stashed into corners and laundry hanging at all angles from the bed frames and overhead lights. There wasn't enough room for any chairs.

For just a moment I can see the ghosts of the men who were confined here, jockeying for a seat on a lower bunk, hunched over, perhaps hanging laundry or trying to sleep, waiting for their hour-a-day out-of-doors. For just a moment I can hear them, laughing or crying, kidding around or fighting, wondering aloud when the hell they were ever going to get out of that place.

The newcomers were required to strip, en masse, for physical exams, and had to use the restrooms in groups and on a schedule. Many were denied mattresses to sleep on. Interrogation was tough, too, and included questions like: *How many windows did your house have? How many steps to your house? Who lived in all the houses surrounding yours?* Interrogations sometimes lasted for days, and immigrants who could not answer the questions to the interrogators' satisfaction were sent back to their country of origin, and had to make the passage at their own expense.

The average length of stay on Angel Island was three-and-a-half weeks, but some immigrants were detained for nearly two years as they waited for their entry papers to be approved. (The average processing time for the twelve million people who entered the United States through Ellis Island, by way of comparison, was just three-and-a-half hours.)

In part, the difficult circumstances were an understandable, although very unfortunate, result of overcrowding. But the Angel Island facility also enforced policies like the Chinese Exclusion Act of 1882, which remained in effect until 1943. As the name indicates, the policy was designed to exclude, rather than embrace, immigrants from China; Americans were afraid Chinese laborers would take their jobs. Of course, Chinese laborers *did* take on jobs—they did backbreaking work in gold and silver mines, were an important source of labor for the transcontinental railroad, and contributed significantly to the economic growth of the American west.

Bestselling author Isabel Allende, herself an immigrant to the United States, is interviewed on the Angel Island Immigration Station website. "Americans want the immigrants, illegal immigrants especially, to do the menial work that nobody else will do," she says. "They want them to do the job in terrible conditions, and then they want them to disappear at six o'clock like ghosts. They don't want to know where they live, how they live.... Just leave them in the shadow like a ghost town, a ghost nation."

Other interviews on the website are equally telling: Dep Chan, who immigrated in 1916, recalls the importance of bribes at the Immigration Station. "As long as you paid, they didn't care.... If you paid ahead of time, you had no problems.... Those who thought their papers were true and didn't bribe got into trouble."

Lena Fong recounts the story of her mother-in-law's seventeen-day stay at Angel Island: "Many people committed suicide in the restroom. She was scared to go. Every day there was someone crying. She felt like those were the worst times of her life."

The Chinese Exclusion Act was the first law preventing a specific ethnic group from immigrating to the United States. It was followed by laws intended to limit the immigration of Japanese, Indian and Filipino people, and was later "strengthened" by the Immigration Act of 1924, which instituted a quota system restricting immigration of Russians, Greeks, Italians, Spanish, Eastern Europeans, Africans, Arabs and East Asians

Another docent elaborated on the suicides. "Even though they were closely guarded, they had methods. Women would put a chopstick in each ear, and then smash them together with both hands. It was that bad."

in an attempt "to preserve the ideal of American homogeneity." It wasn't until 1965 that President Lyndon Johnson signed the provision banning discrimination "in the issuance of an immigrant visa because of the person's race, sex, nationality, place of birth, or place of residence."

As I write this in early 2017, our new president has issued two executive orders to "Protect the Nation from Foreign Terrorist Entry." The first temporarily suspended entry by nationals from seven Muslim-majority countries—Iran, Iraq, Libya, Somalia, Sudan, Syria, and Yemen—and indefinitely suspended the entry of Syrian refugees. The second executive order dropped Iraqi nationals from the list and allowed some exceptions for travelers from the other six countries. Were these executive orders a quirk of fate, or do they signal a new direction for America?

Both executive orders were protested across the United States by citizens who recognized the importance of a diverse population and the dangers of discrimination. And both were obstructed by restraining orders from federal judges contesting their constitutionality.

It was a quirk of fate—and poetry—that led to the preservation of the Angel Island Immigration Station. Closed after a fire in 1940 and slated for demolition in 1970, the detention barracks were preserved because of the discovery of more than two hundred fragments of Chinese poetry carved into their splintered wooden walls. Ranger Alexander Weiss told people about what he saw, and Asian American community members worked to make sure the building was not torn down as had been planned.

Like ghost poems that refuse to leave, the carvings defy layers of paint and plaster, seeping to the surface, testifying to the hopes and fears of the immigrants who passed through. Here's one:

> Living on Island, away from home
>   elicits a hundred feelings.
> My chest is filled with a sadness
>   I cannot bear to explain.
> Night and day, I sit passively and listlessly.
> Fortunately, I have a novel as my companion.

Joe read several of the poems aloud in Chinese, remarking on the attention to rhythm and classical form, the nuanced historical references, and the calligraphers' skill and artistry. Here's another:

> Why should one complain
> If he is detained and imprisoned here?
> From ancient times, heroes often were
> The first ones to face adversity.

The poetry on Angel Island helps to preserve a record of immigration history, but the museum serves an even more important purpose: It reminds us of our national struggle to accept immigrants and embrace ethnic diversity. As Franklin D. Roosevelt, who signed the repeal of the Chinese Exclusion Act, said:

"We are a nation of many nationalities, many races, many religions, bound together by a single unity, the unity of freedom and equality. Whoever seeks to set one nationality against another, seeks to degrade all nationalities. Whoever seeks to set one race against another seeks to enslave all races. Whoever seeks to set one religion against another, seeks to destroy all religion."

Perhaps FDR regretted having issued Executive Order No. 9066, commonly known as the Japanese Internment Act, less than two years earlier. Or perhaps he didn't. Historians have documented Roosevelt's negative opinions about Japanese Americans and Jews. Our "nation of many nationalities" is an imperfect one, still evolving as we work through the awkward and challenging process of acculturation.

As I leave the Immigration Station I stand for a few

minutes, looking out at the sparkling bay and thinking about Joe Chan's parents and all the other immigrants who arrived on this little island. Oddly, spontaneously, I put my right hand over my heart, as though I'm saying the Pledge of Allegiance. I don't even know why I've done this—except that my heart aches for the people who passed through the Immigration Station, people who wanted so badly to come to America.

My visit to this historical site, which is practically in my own backyard, has changed me in the way I always hope travel will: It has expanded my awareness and understanding of another culture. It has helped me empathize with people whose lives are very different from my own. It has made me a better person.

This building in St. Petersburg houses Peter the Great's amazing Cabinet of Curiosities. My better judgement prevented me from including photos of the actual contents. Also, photography was against the rules, and this did not seem like a good place to take a chance on breaking the rules.

The Cabinet of Curiosities

ST. PETERSBURG, RUSSIA

Suspended in clear liquid in a glass jar on the fourth floor of a musty museum in St. Petersburg floats the second strangest thing I have ever seen. It is one strange thing in a whole sea of curiosities, and I feel dizzy. I need to sit down for a moment. There are no chairs in the room, and I don't want to sit on the floor, so I stand and I stare at this oddity for a very long time.

It is a human fetus, but that, in itself, is not what is strange. The tiny fetus is cradled in a hand on the end of the severed arm of a small child. The label describes it as a "foetus about 2 months old in a hand of child about few months old" (sic). A bandage fashioned from a circlet of gauzy white fabric with a frilly lace edge covers the blunt end of the severed forearm. It is gathered and tied with a string, much as a piece of calico cloth might be tied over the lid of a jar of homemade jam.

The lacy edge of the fabric touches just above the wrist, as though it were the hem of the sleeve on a lovely dress. The gauzy cloth is so perfectly proportioned for its use, the delicate lace so expertly applied, the gathering and tying so carefully completed, that I am certain this display was made with a great deal of love.

I look closely. A two-month-old fetus doesn't yet look human. The arms and legs are not well developed, although the vestigal tail has already disappeared. The head is Frankenstein-shaped and disproportionately large, and the ears have not yet migrated up the neck. But I know what it could become, and that knowing fills me with awe. This tiny thing might have grown into a human being. I was this small once. My son must have looked like this. This is every baby.

And then there is the severed arm. The severed arm with the beautiful white sleeve with the delicate lace, that is the second strangest thing I have ever seen. For a moment, I forget to breathe.

I am visiting the Kunstkamera, also called the Museum of Curiosities, officially known as the Peter the Great Museum of Anthropology and Ethnography at the Russian Academy of Sciences. It is housed in a huge old castle with watery-aqua walls and bright white columns that look like frosting on a cake, and it sits on the bank of the roaring Neva River in the heart of St. Petersburg.

Founded by a decree of Tsar Peter the Great for the purpose of "collecting and researching rarities created by nature or man," the museum was opened to the public in 1714. It was said to have been the tsar's favorite part of his grand plan to modernize Russia, which, like much of Europe at that time, still fell under the dark spell of superstition.

Out of ignorance, common people attributed abnormalities to supernatural powers. This superstitious worldview made life particularly difficult for women, who were believed to have consorted with the devil —or at least to have been punished by God for some grave misdeed—if they bore an abnormal child.

In the 1700s thinking progressed from superstition to the popular Theory of Maternal Impression, which proposed that a pregnant woman's mental or emotional state could cause birth defects in her developing infant.

One-hundred-fifty years later the world still believed in the theory of Maternal Impression; Joseph Merrick (1862-1890), the so-called Elephant Man, was a world-famous example. Merrick himself wrote, "The deformity which I am now exhibiting was caused by my mother being ... pushed under the Elephant's feet, which frightened her very much; this occurring during a time of pregnancy was the cause of my deformity."

In one supposed case of Maternal Impression, which was widely publicized, Mary Toft of Surrey, England, was said to have given birth to nine baby rabbits. Mary's persistent dreams of rabbits and her alleged insatiable craving for rabbit meat were said to have influenced the unusual development of her fetuses.

Although her case was eventually exposed as a hoax, Mary Toft, a poor and illiterate woman, made out fairly well. The Duke of Richmond, who lived nearby, took a special interest in Mary, sometimes showing her off to his dinner guests as a curiosity. At the time, extremely large or small people, or those with physical abnormalities, were commonly exhibited across Europe. Many were paid very well.

It was into this milieu, in 1718, that Peter the Great decreed that malformed babies and animals, dead or alive, from across Russia were to be sent to the Kunstkamera. Peter wanted them all, and he would pay for them.

The decree censured "ignoramuses who believe that such monsters are caused by diabolical spells through sorcery and evil eye, which is impossible, because the Creator alone is the god of all creatures, not the Devil," whereas the true reason for malformations is "internal damage as well as fear and the mother's beliefs during pregnancy." The resulting collection was intended to combat prejudices, show the mystery and diversity of nature, and lift proletariat Russia from its superstitious ways. "I want the people to look and learn," the tsar proclaimed.

In the early years of its existence, the Kunstkamera displayed a wide array of anatomical oddities and embalmed anomalies along with rare books, weapons, and seventeenth-century French medical instruments such as forceps and steel probes. It also contained "live exhibits"—children born with physical defects who lived in the Kunstkamera where they were cared for, paid a salary, and displayed to the public.

Today the Kunstkamera is still filled with bizarre things. There are non-human specimens: a taxidermied two-headed calf and a stuffed Indonesian pangolin—an armadillo-sized mammal covered with wide, flat scales—that looks like a gigantic artichoke with legs. There is a hideous, bloated, Jabba-the-Hutt-looking aga toad, native to South America, of particular interest to anthropologists because secretions from its hedonic glands were used to coat the tips of poison arrows.

The secretions from the aga toad's skin are believed to play a role in its sexual attraction and stimulation.

But mostly, there are human specimens, floating in liquid eternity. I saw several examples of conjoined human twins, both skeletal and embalmed, including the Janus-like "Foetus with two faces, occipital conjunction." An extra-large jar held a human head with only one eye, symmetrically positioned in the center of the face—a human Cyclops.

Sadly, baby parts also abound, especially severed arms and legs, most with the lovely lace-edged gauzy bandages, daintily tied. On many of these specimens the tiny fingernails or toenails have been painstakingly painted black, giving them an oddly contemporary Goth feel.

In some cases several specimens are combined into an allegorical display, such as the "Left arm of a few-week-old child: Hand holding fragment of injected placenta" and the "Foot of a child treading on parts of the skull."

Other specimens are more prosaic, such as "Two slices of a penis" or "Knee of a child with dissected joint" or "Two injected kidneys of children, one of them with adrenal."

Most of these incredible pieces are the work of Frederic Ruysch, a Dutch anatomist who met Peter the Great during the tsar's 1697-98 European tour. Ruysch's work was beyond compare. As Chief Instructor officially in charge of Amsterdam's midwives at the turn of the century, he had easy access to stillborn fetuses and aborted embryos, and experimented tirelessly to develop a unique embalming method that produced uncannily lifelike results.

Ruysch never disclosed the formula for the "liquor balsamicum" he used as embalming fluid or his secret technique, which involved injecting the vascular systems of the specimens with red-tinted wax. His astonishingly lifelike results were unmatched for two centuries.

Ruysch's daughter Rachel, a still-life artist, helped her father arrange the displays, "dress" the severed limbs, and decorate the specimens to reflect themes of life's brevity and beauty. They sometimes placed a small gem or a bouquet of flowers in a child's hand, or adorned its head with a crown of bright petals.

Ruysch became widely known for these macabre works of art. In keeping with the vanitas art popular in turn-of-the-century Amsterdam, they were rich in allegory and morbid symbolism, and carried a moral message: Life is beautiful, fragile, and fleeting. Live it well.

Ruysch even established a small personal museum and published catalogs so that ordinary people could become familiar with his collection. The motto at the front of the visitors' book in his museum was *Vene, vidi et judicia nil tuis oculis*, "Come, look, appraise and believe your eyes only."

Ruysch's work was widely admired for years. A century later, when Honoré de Balzac wrote *The*

Magic Skin, his protagonist wandered into a Parisian curiosity shop and encountered the embalmed body of a child, an "enchanting creature," which was one of Ruysch's beautiful preparations.

Kunstkameras, or "curiosity cabinets," holding preparations like Ruysch's as well as other kinds of art, geological specimens, seashells and exotic stuffed animals, were a popular feature of the seventeenth-century palaces of European nobility. Fascinated and inspired by the kunstkameras he saw on his European tour, Peter the Great decided to build his own. He began by purchasing Ruysch's entire collection.

As I am leaving the Kunstkamera I come across another startling specimen and it, too, draws me in so profoundly that I simply stand and stare. It is labeled "Injected specimen of newborn with tail-like appendage and foot teratosis" and it is heartbreaking and horrifying.

It is another human fetus, this time with no decorative lace. The eyes, nose and lips are very clearly defined. The scalp is covered with a fine black fuzz of hair with a clockwise whorl at the crown of the head that looks like a cyclone on a meteorologist's map. The ears are especially well developed, big and fleshy like an old man's. That,

The word *teratosis* comes from a Greek root meaning *monster.*

along with the fetus's wrinkly face and slightly worried expression, give it an odd air of knowingness.

But that is the end of its humanness. Its eyes, unopened, tilt up toward the outside, the way intergalactic aliens' eyes are often depicted. It has only one leg, a small one, a little smaller than its arm, with what looks like a thumb growing off the heel. Its most startling aspect is the beginning of a large tail, longer than the child's ear and thicker, more bulbous, like a knee or a shoulder. This creature—which barely seems human—is even stranger than the fetus in the hand of a child, stranger than the lace-clad severed arms, or the human Cyclops or the two-headed calf.

My dizziness returns. All this deformity has transported me to a neverland of fascination and revulsion, a house of mirrors with unsettling questions around every corner. Heartbreak, humiliation, terror, blame, curiosity—these emotions must have been as disorienting to those long-ago viewers as they are to me now.

The Kunstkamera was an early look into the mysteries of creation and its science. But of course the situation is even more complicated. Today we can create—*we are creating*—chimeras in the lab. Researchers are already performing experiments that insert human stem cells into animal embryos—

experiments that could eventually provide "human" organs for transplant—that take the mysteries of creation into strange, new, and sometimes terrifying terrain. The Kunstkamera is not just a collection of curiosities. It is a vivid reminder of the moral complexities we face, complexities that once defied the imagination, complexities that will become ever more tortuous as we attempt to understand—and expand—what it means to be human.

The image above, titled "Chaman Amazonie" and courtesy of Wikimedia, is pretty much what I expected an Amazonian shaman to look like. He looks nothing—I repeat, nothing—like the shaman I met.

WHAT THE SHAMAN SAW

BUZIOS, BRAZIL

I have always wanted to meet a shaman. A lover of plants and wildlife, I'm impressed with the shaman's understanding and use of those realms, with his abilities to tease remarkable experiences from the natural world. I remember when the *Don Juan* books came out: *The Teachings of Don Juan, A Separate Reality, Journey to Ixtlan*, and many more. I was impressed. Author Carlos Castaneda's journey resonated deeply with me—even if I didn't believe all the details. His mysterious message—that there are hidden ways of seeing the world—made me feel deliciously insignificant, like the ocean or the mountains do for many people. It also aroused a deep fascination with the relationship between spirituality and the natural world.

For years I harbored a secret desire to travel to a faraway land and learn from a medicine man myself. So when, decades later, I had an opportunity to meet a Brazilian shaman—*a real shaman!*—I jumped at the chance. I was with a group of international students who had traveled to Buzios, Brazil, to study rainforest ecology for six weeks. I had studied indigenous medicinal plants in California and Argentina; this experience in Brazil would broaden my perspective. But the best part was that our American instructor, Amanda, had arranged for a local shaman to work with us during our stay.

Of course, we were not going on a spiritual quest, but I was excited just to meet a real shaman. I wanted to learn what plants he used and how he prepared them. Also, I admit, I was curious about how a shaman lived his daily life. I wanted to see the world through his eyes.

Amanda hadn't told us very much about the healer—only that he was a "great shaman" and that he "worked with the people." Somehow, during six anticipatory months, I had created an image in my mind of a wild, native medicine man wearing very little clothing, with a large rattle in his right hand and a golden mane-like headdress that brought to mind the endangered golden tamarind lion monkeys living in this rainforest. Excitement does that to me sometimes.

The man I finally met was wearing plenty of clothing. In fact, he looked quite stylish in an expensive suit and beautiful shoes. His right hand generally held a cell phone or a laser pointer—not a rattle. The shaman's name was Antonio, and he was going to teach us all about rainforest plants.

Antonio was handsome. His eyes and hair were black, his skin was warm brown, and his lips were full and fleshy. He looked like Antonio Banderas. All day, as Amanda translated, Antonio spoke to us in his musical Portuguese about the plants, about energies, about the origins of disease. "*E importante usar ervas selvagens* ... It is important to use wild—not cultivated—herbs for healing, because sometimes it's the stress of competition that produces the active ingredient in the plant."

What an interesting idea! I wondered whether this law from the plant kingdom might have a corollary in the human world. It reminded me of studies I'd read about that suggest super-achieving adult athletes are such high performers in part *because of* a certain amount of emotional stress at a particular stage of childhood.

"Sickness is not a punishment; each person has a responsibility for his or her own health. God is not preoccupied with whether we are good or bad people. It is not the soil's responsibility what is planted in it ..."

On and on they went for an entire day, with Antonio instructing us in his understanding of the way the world works and Amanda translating. "Consider the planet a living organism, with thoughts and feelings," Antonio explained. "Climate is the earth's emotions. Amino acids, carbohydrates, etcetera, are not what generates life; they are the materialization of life."

I admit, I was having a hard time understanding what was metaphorical and what was meant to be understood literally. "Do you mean that lightning created life?" I asked. That could make sense; in fact, it fit quite nicely, and reminded me of one of the theories we'd studied in high-school biology class, that lightning sparked inorganic molecules to create amino acids, which eventually resulted in RNA and then DNA. "Is lightning a metaphor for the Earth's emotion?"

"No, no!" Antonio insisted. "None of it is metaphor. The earth's emotions are what generate life. Where they meet and interact, they generate life."

I had no clue what Antonio meant. Perhaps by asking more questions I would eventually understand. "What about people—how do we fit in?" I responded.

"Imagine we are fish, living in a sea of energy. In the sea, there are fish created by the sea, living in the sea, part of the food chain. The fish will eventually die and become part of the sea, and then new fish again."

I remained confused. "So are you saying that there is some energy that is greater than our selves, something that lasts even after our individual consciousnesses have died?" Maybe Antonio was talking about reincarnation.

His answer was frustratingly indirect. "Think of mind as broadcast information," he explained. "The brain is like a TV to receive it."

I still didn't get it, but at the end of the first day I shook Antonio's hand appreciatively and thanked him for the class. Then he did a very odd thing. He invited me to accompany him to a friend's birthday party that evening.

"But we don't speak the same language," I protested to Amanda, who was standing nearby. "Will you come along to translate?"

"No, no," Antonio interrupted. "I am not asking Amanda. I am asking you." Apparently he *did* understand a little English. And apparently a translating chaperone was not what he'd had in mind.

Intrigued with the idea of getting to know this healer better, I decided to go along to his friend's party. I know five words of Portuguese (*bom, dia, selva, obrigado,* and *vegetariano*) and I felt extremely awkward, but the people there were friendly and I was taking the first step toward understanding foreign ideas, language, culture and people. For example, at dinner that evening I learned that Antonio was a vegetarian—as was I, pretty much. I've always eaten very little meat because I prefer other foods, but Antonio avoided meat for a very different reason.

The next morning, with Amanda to translate, Antonio explained his vegetarianism. "Mammals have memories," Antonio said. If you eat mammals, you eat their memories. It's the same with fish and fowl. Plants also have memories, but they are very different from our own, and so do not affect us."

"What happens when you eat the memories?" I asked.

"When I eat the bodies of animals, I experience very unpleasant memories in my own body."

I wondered whether there was a relationship between the adrenalin in the animal's body and these memories. Maybe Antonio was super-sensitive to adrenalin-drenched meat. "Is kosher killing any different, in terms of the memories? If the death is quick and painless, the meat wouldn't contain all those awful death memories, would it?" I asked.

Amanda and Antonio had a quick conversation about the meaning of the word "kosher," then Antonio said that kosher didn't make any difference. I thought that if Amanda had to explain the word then probably

Antonio wasn't familiar with the process, so he could not really answer the question. When I pressed he said he understood the process, but had not known the word in English. I decided that perhaps the memories we eat—and which subsequently trouble Antonio— are *all* the animal's memories, not just death memories. That would explain why kosher killing didn't make a difference.

Day after day, Antonio spoke and Amanda translated. And day after day I asked questions, doggedly trying to understand.

"Memories reside physically in our bodies, not in our brains," Antonio explained. The brain tells you *where* in the body a memory resides."

"Do all parts of our bodies hold memories?" I asked.

"Most female experiences reside in the genital region. It has to do with being a mother, with the kinds of responsibilities a woman has—not with sexual function. Male experiences tend to reside in the chest, for the same reason."

And so it went for days. In the classroom, Antonio explained his understanding of health and sickness, balance and responsibility, mind and emotion. In the field, we learned to identify *alacrim du praia, capoeiraba branca, espinheira santa, ponta libre, guine pipiao*—more than fifty medicinal herbs in all. We learned to dry them, grind them and mix them into capsules and infusions. We learned to listen to the herbs and to respect them.

One evening, after we knew each other a little better, I commented that Antonio spoke English with a Chinese accent. I would never have said it, if I'd known how embarrassed he'd get. Antonio explained that he'd learned his little bit of English while studying Chinese medicine, which he found to be a good fit with his own interests and skills. He was an acupuncture practitioner, and Chinese philosophy had influenced him deeply.

"Lao Tse says the bowl is made of clay. The clay is the substance; the empty space is the essence. So it is with us; our empty space is our essence."

I liked the idea about substance and essence, but it frustrated me. It was so beautiful, so simple and elegant, and yet its truth eluded me so completely that I was certain I would never understand. How can my empty space be my essence?

In class, we continued to ask Antonio questions, and after a few days he told us about the rainbow-colored worms he had seen since childhood. "One day I was playing at a friend's house, and I saw a very large worm coming out of my friend's mother's back. I

204

asked about it, but my friend and his mother did not know what I meant. A short time later, I learned that the mother had lung cancer."

"Do you 'see' the worms like you see the chair I am sitting on?" I asked.

"Yes and no. I see it clearly, as a real thing, not a metaphor. But I have to look for it in order to see it."

"Is it like paying attention?"

"Yes."

Now we were getting somewhere. "Are the worms like auras?" I knew a little bit about auras, at least in theory. I had even taken a class once, to try to learn to see them.

"No, they are not like auras," Antonio said.

So much for that line of questioning. "Are they real or do you just have a feeling about them?"

"They are real."

"Why is it that you can see them and I cannot?"

"I don't know." He tried another explanation.

"Picture concentric circles. The virus lives in the central circle, in the realm of the physical. The worms live in the next circle out. Next comes emotion, then mental energy. Karma is the outside part."

"So viruses and bacteria *cause* disease, and the worms are a manifestation of it?"

"Viruses and bacteria are not the causative agent of

disease. They just take advantage of an already-existing weakness, which was caused by an internal or external entity ... which *also* was just taking advantage of an existing situation. The causes of disease can be internal or external. Pay attention. It is important for the interior consciousness to have a good, neighborly relationship with the consciousness outside."

"What *are* the causes then, if they are not bacteria and viruses?"

"Internal causes are our emotions. External causes are climate, nutrition and lifestyle. Anything else is a complication. Both internal and external causes have their own intelligence, their own way to live, their own consciousness, their own way to create things."

"What about what we call infectious diseases?"

"Diseases that affect whole communities are about the community; they are not about the virus. They show what is happening with the community. They are like flies—everyone complains about them, but they are around because of the garbage the community throws out."

"How do mental diseases like depression and schizophrenia fit in?" I asked, curious about these two problems that had had a deep impact on my own family.

"Depression is energy. The family sends the energy out through the individual. The whole family must be treated. Schizophrenia is the result of genetic garbage, a fertile ground for many weaknesses to manifest."

"How do you treat the disease? Does treatment have to do with the worms?"

"It is not necessary to treat the worms; the weakness that they took advantage of must be strengthened. Acupuncture works well when there are lots of worms. When there is only mucous—no worms yet—it works better to use nutritional plants for treatment."

I couldn't stop wondering about Antonio's worms. Why couldn't I understand what they were all about? Maybe it was as though I were deaf, and questioning him about sound—no matter what he answered, it would be incomprehensible to me. I wondered whether I had any worms, and, if so, whether Antonio would tell me about them. Would I even want to know about my own worms? What if I had big, nasty, well developed ones? What if Antonio gave me bad news?

Finally I decided, *Yes, I would want to know.* I was curious to find out what Antonio saw when he looked at me. So I screwed up my courage and asked, "Antonio, would you look to see whether I have any worms?"

Three other students, Robert, Kathy and Ellen, overheard. They, too, wanted "readings," and Antonio agreed to look for our worms. That evening we sat together in a quiet corner of the classroom.

Antonio saw things we could not see. He saw a swimming pool in my leg and pulled out a worm of fear. He saw a small red convertible in Robert's groin. He saw a grey English city in Ellen's chest—some deep, unspeakable pain—and she cried for an hour.

Antonio could not have known—not in any normal way—that I'd been afraid of swimming pools for many years, ever since my brother and I were playing around in one and he'd held me underwater for a little too long. He could not have known that Rob and Kathy were trying to have a child, but had been unable to conceive; a specialist had recently told them that something was wrong with Rob's testicles, probably due to an injury he had sustained years ago in an automobile accident. The car he was driving at the time was a small red convertible. Antonio could not have known about Ellen's secret pain, and neither he nor Ellen ever revealed the details to the rest of us.

"Antonio," I asked once he'd read us all, "Have you always seen the worms, or did you learn to see them, or did something happen to you and then you could see them?"

"I have always seen them. As a child, I assumed that everyone else could see them too, and this caused some confusing communications. Eventually I realized that other people could not see the worms, and then I stopped talking about them."

In the evenings, Antonio and I continued to talk. I wanted to learn as much as I could, and Antonio wanted to practice English, which he didn't dare attempt in front of the class. I could understand why. It would have taken forever. He could not have been precise, and he would have sounded dumb, although in fact he was both intelligent and well educated. Antonio had a law degree, but didn't practice law. Healing was his calling.

Over the weeks we had together I asked Antonio many questions. Often I felt odd about it, and wondered what it would feel like to be constantly peppered with questions from someone whose worldview was so different from my own that I had to explain even the most basic concepts.

In time Antonio questioned me, too. "There are four types of people who seek divine understanding," he told me at one point. "Intellectuals, the devout, the seriously ill, and people who want money. What are your motives?"

My motives? Why was he asking me this? Was I taking up too much of his time? Was I asking too many questions? "Well, I'm not ill and I have no illusions about making money as a healer. I'm not an intellectual, either, although I'm very curious. But I do have a deep spiritual yearning. So I guess that means I am devout, although I'm not religious."

"Creating harmony between yourself and the earth or a power place is the work of magic," he responded cryptically. "The earth's energy can kill people if it is not harmonized. Doing the work is easy, but staying in harmony is very hard; it makes some people go mad."

"How does religion fit in?"

"Religions are effective when they are very clear and specific about rules, when they draw lines clearly for us. Philosophy without religion is mental disturbance; religion without philosophy is stupidity."

Eventually I learned about Antonio's own motives for trying to understand healing and the nature of disease: He was seriously ill. He had a hereditary autoimmune disease with a long name—I can't remember it—that caused lots of big lumps underneath his skin. He'd had it since childhood, and periodically went to a medical center for treatment.

I knew it must be insensitive, but I had to ask, "How can a healer be ill? Can't you just heal yourself?"

"Yes, and I do—some. But it is a very powerful disease. And healing, like disease, is an ongoing process."

So is understanding, I'd venture to add. Perhaps

some day I will understand how viruses and worms and karma are related, how to create harmony between myself and the earth. And when that day comes—*if* that day comes—I might even understand what the shaman saw.

I came across this statue in a park in Brazil; it perfectly depicts the terrifying Amazonian serpents I expected to encounter on my Ayahuasca trip, except that I figured the ones that visited me would probably be a lot bigger than this.

SISTER SERPENT, BROTHER BEAR
A SECRET LOCATION IN NORTHERN CALIFORNIA

The room swirls as I struggle to control my nausea. Psychedelic colors and shapes fly under rainforest umbrellas with fluid snakes, inherent leaves, crazy sparkles! I want to enjoy all these wild, beautiful images, but as soon as one comes it is replaced by another, and then another, and another, as though I am watching television and someone else has the remote control and they are changing the channels so fast I can't register one image before it is replaced by the next, and the next, and the next, so what could have been beautiful is actually frantic and feverish and intensely annoying. And it's been going on for hours.

Let me explain how I ended up on the floor of a stranger's house, shaking a rattle and facing my own private serpents with a singing shaman. I have to go back a ways, to when I was fifteen. That's when I first read about a plant preparation called ayahuasca, which, when ingested, somehow creates a direct connection between the user and the natural world. It is used in religious ceremonies by indigenous people in the Amazon, whose discovery of the brew seems unbelievably improbable.

Ayahuasca is a combination of two rainforest plants—two specific plants from among the 80,000 Amazonian plant species. One plant happens to contain a hormone, dimethyltryptamine (DMT), that occurs naturally in many mammals—including humans—and can induce hallucinations. DMT has been called "the most hardcore psychedelic drug known to man." The other plant contains a substance that inactivates an enzyme in our digestive tracts that would otherwise block the effects of the DMT. The two plants need to be boiled together for several hours before they work in concert as ayahuasca. How on earth did "primitive" people discover this? Amazonian shamans say that the plants speak to them—their knowledge comes directly from the plants themselves.

I never dreamed I'd be able to try this rainforest sacrament, but I fervently wanted to; it's been on my bucket list since before I even knew what a bucket list was. I have felt a connection with the divine many times, and it's always been initiated by a feeling of awe in the presence of nature. The direct connection ayahuasca promised seemed like the closest one could come to a direct connection with God.

Years later I read a book, *The Cosmic Serpent:*

DNA and the Origins of Knowledge, by Jeremy Narby, that described how the author's graduate work in ethnobotany led him to work with people who used ayahuasca as a sacrament. Narby had an elaborate theory about DNA being the conduit for direct, transspecies communication, beginning with the fact that DNA itself does not change from species to species; only the order of its components varies. His line of reasoning extended, eventually, to the idea that ayahuasca allows shamans to take their consciousnesses down to a molecular level where they can communicate directly with DNA—with life itself.

Only the order of DNA's components varies. That's why the biotech industry exists: Scientists can, for example, extract the snippet of human DNA that holds instructions for making insulin and insert it into the DNA of a bacterium, which will then produce something very similar to human insulin—the DNA's message has been carried from one species to another.

The way Narby presented those ideas blew my mind, and reawakened that long-time desire to try ayahuasca. I started asking around, quietly, and discovered I knew someone who knew someone who knew someone who conducted ayahuasca ceremonies. They were not legal in California where I lived. An appointment was arranged.

First, Ramon interviewed me on the phone, then we met in person. Ramon wanted to make sure I was interested in ayahuasca for spiritual reasons, not because I wanted to trip out. I'd never had any particular interest in hallucinogens back in the LSD-laced hippie days, but that changed as spirituality became more and more important in my life. Hallucinogens can, of course, create the feeling of being moved or finding something extremely meaningful—the same feeling we associate with spiritual experiences. I was curious about the relationship between hallucinogens and spirituality.

I had another reason to be interested. My younger brother suffered from schizophrenia, a devastating illness that left him unable to function in the real world. He was lost to us, wandering in some strange, alternate universe of bizarre ideas. One of schizophrenia's effects on my brother was an unshakeable belief that certain, seemingly random events held secret spiritual messages for him. Once, for example, he determined—based on stringing together the final words in a dozen films he had recently watched—that God was telling him to visit the actress Cher. He made it as far as the outdoor swimming pool at her Malibu home, which he apparently enjoyed for several hours before an officer of the law hauled him off to a holding cell. The sensation of extreme "meaningfulness" common in schizophrenic break-down is apparently similar to the one elicited by hallucinogens, and I wanted to understand more about it.

When it's working properly, the attribution of meaningfulness is essential for our everyday lives. It helps us determine which events are most important to remember—such as *The fire burned my hand*, or *That wheel sure does save time*. So it's no surprise we've evolved with powerful neurotransmitters that create such feelings.

I guess I passed Ramon's interview, because he handed me an eleven-page instructional document detailing preparation for the ceremony. It emphasized universal love, working for the greater good, and the importance of purity of purpose. "Effects vary tremendously depending upon diet, preparation, and intention," the instructions said. Ramon also handed me a list of things I could and could not eat for ten days prior to the ayahuasca ceremony.

"The diet is strict; do you think you can stick to it?" he asked.

I reviewed the list. I could eat rice and vegetables. I was also allowed small amounts of fish or chicken, broiled, steamed or grilled. "Hmmm. No salt, spices or other seasonings," I read, a bit apprehensively.

"Also, no yeast, fatty foods, citrus fruits, pickles, green peppers or jam," Ramon pointed out. "No dairy products, soy products, figs, raisins, chocolate, alcohol, tobacco, or caffeine. No aged protein, salad dressing, sugar, snails, pickled herring, garlic, or chili peppers.

Can you do that?"

"No problem, Ramon. I can definitely do it." I didn't want to sound unsure, or give Ramon a reason to kick me out of the program.

My confidence was premature, however. The pickled herring and snails were not a problem, but I do live in America, and many of the forbidden foods would be hard to avoid for ten days. As far as I'm concerned salt, fat and caffeine are the three major food groups. And eliminating bread and cheese meant forgoing daily staples.

I wondered how much of this diet was really a physical preparation, and how much was psychological. No matter. Sometimes, in the realm of the spirit, it's important to do things simply because they are part of the process, regardless of whether or not they seem to make sense.

I managed to adhere to the diet almost perfectly, mainly because I was afraid of what might happen if I didn't. Ramon had explained that many of the forbidden foods were high in tyrosine—an amino acid that affects the same neural pathways as the ayahuasca's active ingredients do—and could therefore mess with my neural metabolism during the ceremony. Others would cause severe nausea. Both results seemed worth going to some degree of trouble to avoid.

Ramon also asked me to bring a rattle, and explained how to prepare the special ritual arrow I would need for the ceremony. The location of the event was a secret, revealed only at the last minute. Ramon emailed directions the day before our ceremony was to take place, and the next afternoon I drove through a deep forest to a comfortable ranch-style home—donated by its owners for this express purpose for twenty-four hours. There were only seven of us, plus Ramon and a helper.

"I will conduct the ceremony," Ramon explained. "That means I will drink the ayahuasca myself. Ayesha, my helper, has participated in the ceremony several times, but tonight she will not participate. She will be available in case you need help going to the bathroom, and she can call a doctor if anyone needs medical assistance."

I was glad someone was going to stay straight, but *Ayesha*? Why did she have to have such a New-Age name? Also, being reminded that any of us could require medical attention at any time didn't put my mind at ease.

I began to worry. And then I began to fear that worrying was not a good thing. Ayahuasca was supposed to get us in touch with the core of our true selves, to reveal our primal strengths and fears. What if my true core was worry? Worse yet, what if it was fear? Would I be frightened out of my mind by the experience?

Much of what I've read about people's ayahuasca visions involved interactions with gigantic, terrifying dragons, for a reason that apparently has to do with the snake-like double helix structure of DNA. From what I could tell, horrifying snake and dragon images seemed to be an essential aspect of the ayahuasca experience. Would the dragons visit me? Would I be able to tolerate the intense fear? Would the ayahuasca trigger a psychological breakdown and if so, what would that mean—would I join my brother in his inescapable alternate universe? I wanted to learn something essential about myself, but didn't want to lose myself forever in the process.

One of the other participants—I'll call him Ralph—brought a cozy-looking sheepskin rug to sit on. I wished I'd thought of that. I even had one at home. He also brought a fancy metal bowl that looked like it had come from Tibet to puke—I mean *purge*—into. I didn't think to bring accoutrements that would make this a *fancy* occasion. In fact, I'd dressed down—blue jeans and a T-shirt, and a cozy old purple sweater that had already been through the wash quite a few times. The ceremony was going to take hours. I wanted to be comfortable, and didn't want to worry about throwing up on nice clothes. I was resigned to the fact that I *would* throw up. Almost everyone did, Ramon had explained. And since I get motion sickness quite easily, I just accepted that the experience would involve at least one good upchuck. I hoped the results would be worth it.

Ralph, it turned out, was not a first-timer; he'd participated in several ayahuasca ceremonies and acted like he knew exactly what he was doing. Ralph wore brightly colored hippie clothes: orange patterned pants, a blue tie-dye shirt and a leather vest with long fringe. This guy was ready to trip. I wondered how he'd made it past Ramon's interview. Ralph's rattle was brightly colored, too, and looked like he'd bought it in an import store. Fancy. Ralph explained that he hadn't bothered to adhere to the pre-ceremony diet this time. He apparently thought it was just for beginners.

He also had not spent much time on his ceremonial arrow; it was an ordinary stick, sharpened on one end like a giant pencil and with a piece of bright red yarn tied around the other end. It seemed at once too plain and too gaudy for the circumstances. Ralph definitely hadn't spent enough time preparing it. I was sure that would impact his experience negatively, and was glad I had taken great care with making my own arrow. But then again, I hadn't dressed up. Maybe that would be some kind of signal—To my inner self? To the universe?—that I didn't care enough to take the ceremony seriously. Would the dragons mind if I wasn't dressed quite right?

We sat in a circle on the living room floor. Ralph sat across from me on his fuzzy sheepskin rug, and I perched on a little throw pillow. In front of me were my rattle, my ceremonial arrow and the big stainless steel mixing bowl I'd brought for the inevitable nausca. I admired Ralph's Tibetan bowl.

We went around the circle, introducing ourselves briefly: sharing our reasons for being there, expressing gratitude for the opportunity to touch the spiritual world, and mentioning any past experiences with hallucinogens. Ralph went last, and directed one of his comments at me. "Wow, you are *so* brave! I can't believe your first experience with hallucinogens is going to be with ayahuasca, the granddaddy of them all. You've never even dropped acid?"

I searched for a response, but only came up with a lame, "Yeah, thanks. I mean, no, I haven't, but thanks; I guess I *am* brave." What I was thinking was, *Thanks a lot, Ralph. That's just what I need right now— another reason to stress out. This was not supposed to be about bravery, was it? I'm pretty sure that's*

222

not one of my strengths. And I drifted off in a sea of worry.

Next Ramon played music on a wooden flute and we accompanied him with our rattles. Then he chanted for a long time. He had one puff on a cigarette—I couldn't see the brand—and then extinguished it. He splashed ceremonial water on himself and sang four or five lovely, melodic songs in a language I had never heard. We sat silently until Ramon finished singing.

Then, one at a time, each of us stood and walked over to Ramon, where he blessed us with ceremonial cigarette smoke. He sang a short song for each of us in turn. Then he offered the ayahuasca. We drank it from little blue Dixie cups with white flowers on them.

The ayahuasca preparation is commonly referred to as a "tea," which suggested to me that it would ladies as an afternoon pick-me-up—thin, warm, and fragrant. But this was nothing like tea. It was the vilest stuff I'd ever tasted. Bitter as dragon's bile, it also had elements of burnt garbage, rotted vegetables, stagnant pond water and a hint of prune juice. It *looked* like prune juice, dark and thick, with lots of fiber. I felt the nausea almost immediately, and I think it lasted about an hour, but I never threw up. Ralph was not so fortunate.

My perception of time changed—hours passed in what seemed like only minutes. I saw psychedelic images: bright colors, crazy animals, juicy-luscious-bursting blossoms and petals and vines—flower-power images that were remarkably similar to posters I'd had on my bedroom wall in the early '70s. It gave me a whole new appreciation for those psychedelic images—*now I knew where they came from.*

Or did I? I remember wondering whether they arose from my memory or my imagination, or somewhere outside myself—perhaps the place where the snakes lived. Most of the images were so different from anything I had ever seen that I was certain they were not memories. And my imagination could never have conjured them up, either—especially not that fast. *Inventiveness and endless variety, internal coherence, definitely a sense of humor, pattern, color, beauty, vapor, swirling movement*—they all flashed at me at a million miles an hour, as though I was watching the coolest TV show ever, but someone kept changing the channel, and the next show was just as good, but before I could even register it the channel changed again, and on and on for hours.

I do remember three specific images. I saw snakes, rather than dragons. Very small snakes. They were illustrated critters, colorful and quite beautiful, the kind of creatures that might wiggle across the parchment of an illuminated manuscript. The snakes were almost cute—certainly not scary—and I wished they would stay around longer.

I also saw a group of about a dozen men in black robes with peaked black hoods that covered their faces. I understood quite clearly, telepathically, that the men were menacing and that I should be afraid, but I wasn't. They were just guys in black robes—almost like Halloween costumes, but not quite. Almost laughable, but not quite.

Finally, I saw a huge grizzly bear in a silent, snowy evergreen forest. The grizzly was standing up on its hind legs and was right in front of me, so close I couldn't see its head—just its immense, muscular body, long brown fur, and the old wooden sled it clasped tightly to its chest.

When I asked Ramon later what the images might have meant, he wasn't much help. "Maybe the ayahuasca was showing you that things that seem frightening really aren't so bad after all," he suggested. *Maybe,* I thought. *But what about the bear that was going sledding? What did that mean? Wasn't I supposed to learn something from the creatures I met?*

I had read that if a creature approaches you in a dream or a vision you should greet it and ask it what it wants. But I hadn't had the presence of mind to ask the bear anything while I was with it, so that wasn't an option. Instead, I looked up "bear" in a dream dictionary, but its suggestions—feelings about being a solitary creature; danger of sudden unpredictable responses; feelings of threat—didn't ring true. They didn't grab at my heart or my gut, so I doubted they were the explanation I was looking for.

I had given up hope of figuring out what the bear meant, and in fact had forgotten about the question entirely, when I got my answer—months later—in an unexpected way. I was reading an article and came across the phrase, "like those bears in your dreams that chase you over and over again, never catching you but never stopping either..." It was written as though that were a meme: *Bears that chase you in your dreams but never catch you.* When I read it I suddenly remembered my ayahuasca bear. And there it was, out of the blue, the unmistakable feeling of *meaningfulness* I had been seeking.

I knew *this* was the message I was meant to get: *That the bear—something that seemed dangerous—simply wanted to play in the snow. The bear, the "serpents," even the men in black hoods: They weren't fearsome enemies; they were my brothers and sisters.* Ramon was right, but I'd needed to figure out the message—to experience it—for myself.

I knew this was the right interpretation of the bear's message because it *felt* right. I trusted that feeling and my own ability to pay attention to it, identify it, and interpret it. My ayahuasca tea party was long past, but that rush of meaningfulness connected me to the spirit world, to my own intuitive capabilities—and, in a profound way, to my lost little brother.

SPECIAL **FLYING SAUCER** ISSUE!...See Page 4

AMAZING

STORIES

OCTOBER 35¢

IS THE GOVERNMENT HIDING SAUCER FACTS?
Raymond Palmer Says, Yes!

"OUTER SPACE SAUCERS—A MYTH!"
By Oliver P. Ferrell

"THE ALIENS ARE AMONG US!"
By Gray Barker

Richard Shaver
Rev. Neal Harvey
Many Others

A key part of Dad's theory about aliens is their dissemination of disinformation in a way that integrates a belief in alien visitors into our popular culture.

THEY'VE SEEN THE SAUCERS
EARTH

I've seen them. I've been there with them.
I can tell you all you want to know.

— Elton John and Bernie Taupin,
"I've Seen the Saucers"

More than one hundred retired military men sit together in a conference room, looking like ordinary American husbands, fathers and grandfathers. They are rigorously trained, disciplined, and proud to have served their country. They have no difficulty differentiating fact from fiction. And they share a startling secret.

It's a secret they have not been able to talk about for the past fifty years. They have not been able to discuss it with their colleagues or their wives or the press, and certainly not with their superior officers. But they have not stopped thinking about it—not for half a century. They cannot stop thinking about it. It's the kind of thing that lurks in the back of their minds, bursting out in dreams or nightmares, coloring everything they think about. Sometimes it even makes them question their own sanity.

They've all seen flying saucers.

And they have all taken action. These men have joined an organization called MUFON—the Mutual UFO Network—in order to investigate UFO sightings, discuss evidence, debunk disinformation, and, perhaps most of all, to connect with each other. I attended their annual conference one summer in Denver with my dad. He's been a MUFON member for years because he saw a UFO once, and it changed his life. It was many years ago, on a dark highway in rural Colorado, where we were on a family vacation. I was a small child at the time, and don't remember it.

But Dad cannot forget. A bright light appeared in the sky behind our car. Dad saw it first in the rearview mirror. As he tells the story, it came from high in the sky and approached the car quickly—far faster than a jet plane would be capable of moving. It was also much brighter than anything he'd ever seen. The light paused for a few seconds behind our car, and then it disappeared. It didn't fly away—it didn't *go* anywhere—it simply disappeared.

A retired banker and one-time math and science

teacher who wrote his master's thesis on instructional methodology in astronomy, my father is not prone to flights of fancy. He does not drink or smoke. His idea of fun is looking through a telescope or a microscope or going scuba diving—all alternative ways of looking at the universe, now that I think about it.

Dad became so involved with MUFON that he worked his way up to being the Principle Investigator for the state of Iowa, where we lived. His responsibilities included investigating reports of UFO sightings, which meant he interviewed people who had seen UFOs, or who *thought* they had. His job was to document what they had seen, when they had seen it, whether they were wearing their eyeglasses at the time, how big the object was, how it moved around, and all the details they could remember. Then he checked multiple sources for records of weather balloons, airplanes, saucer-like cloud formations and other potential explanations.

Sometimes he investigated incidents in which a person seemed to have been abducted by space aliens. In these cases he asked questions about where the person was, who they were with, what they had been doing, whether they had ever had any mental health problems, whether they had been drinking or using any kind of drugs—even an allergy medication—how much time had elapsed during the incident, and, of course, what had happened during that time.

I am attending this conference reluctantly—because Dad asked me to come and I'm trying to be a good daughter—not because I believe in UFOs. Well, let me clarify. I do believe there are objects that appear to fly and are as yet unidentified. So in that sense, yes, I believe in unidentified flying objects—UFOs. But I doubt that they belong to extraterrestrial beings visiting us from outer space. So in that sense, no, I probably don't believe in UFOs. But I'm amazed at the people who do.

The men—they're almost all men—participating in this conference seem like regular people. They are not Post Traumatic Stress Disorder veterans. They are not homeless people who roam the streets; they are not suffering from addictions or substance abuse problems or the inability to hold down a job. Many of them are retired from distinguished careers at places like GE, Westinghouse, Rockwell International, McDonnell-Douglas, and the Federal Aviation Administration. Together, they have excelled at a daunting assignment: staying silent for their entire careers about classified U.S. military incidents. Much of this information is fifty years old and has recently been declassified, which makes this year's MUFON convention especially exciting. Even so, the tone of the conference is serious—almost somber. And the men remain reticent about sharing what they saw. It's difficult to begin talking about things you've been actively suppressing for fifty years. And yet here they are, wanting—needing—to connect with one another.

At the conference, I'm forced to take another look at my father. "Dad, explain to me again why this makes any sense at all," I begin, as we sit together on gray metal folding chairs in the crowded conference room, waiting for the next presentation to begin. We've had this conversation several times, and I love the way his theory explains so much. Even more, I love the way his voice takes on a slight urgency when he talks about UFOs.

"Well, first of all, you have to think about it from the aliens' perspective," Dad begins. This might be the only place in the world he can utter a sentence like that in public without fear of being overheard. I try to imagine how that must feel.

"By definition, they must be part of a civilization that is technologically much more advanced than ours. And it only makes sense that if they have been around long enough to be this technologically advanced, they're probably advanced in other ways, too, like sociologically. They've got to be giving some consideration to what it would do to humanity to suddenly discover that we aren't alone in the universe."

This is a favorite topic of Dad's, and many other attendees, too. Disclosure. Why does the government refuse to disclose the truth of UFOs to the public? When will they finally do so? What will force their hand? And, even more important, how will the world react? What will happen to religion? What will happen to the stock market? What will happen to governments when it becomes clear they have no control over the aliens?

The topic of disclosure is central to Dad's theories about UFOs. "The aliens realize that we'll need a long time to get accustomed to the idea that they're out there. They know it will be tremendously disruptive, and they are probably wise enough to realize the immorality of interfering with another planet's civilizations. That's why they plant so much disinformation."

"Why would they plant disinformation? Wouldn't they want us to know the truth?"

"Yes, but the knowledge would be too much for us to handle all at once. That's why they have introduced the idea as a sort of folklore, not really believable, but part of popular culture all around the world. Your Elton John even sings about it." Dad referred to all musical artists from the '60s onwards as "yours" because they were clearly not his. He's never had any interest in "my" music, and I'm surprised he even knows Elton John's name. "They're insinuating themselves into music and TV shows so people aren't shocked by the idea when disclosure finally happens."

Talking about disclosure in this way seems oddly religious, like talking about the Rapture. Not that I would know; the Rapture has never been a topic of conversation at Mom and Dad's dinner table. But there does seem to be an eerie similarity: Each is imminent yet completely out of our control. And each will change everything.

"UFOs are saucer-shaped or they're cigar-shaped or they're shapeless bright lights or they're orbs," Dad reminds me. "Sometimes they appear in tight triangular formation and other times they're in a trapezoid. Sometimes they disappear into thin air. It's all done to confuse us. No one is sure what they are, but everyone has heard of them. The aliens have been preparing us for a long time."

"So then is it the government, or the aliens, that are spreading disinformation?" It feels odd to be questioning my father like this, as though he is some crazy conspiracy theorist. I do my best to remain open to his ideas.

"It's both, but I doubt that they're doing it together. They each have their own reasons. But think about it: We elect a new president every four years, and with all he has to do, I don't think every new president of the United States is going to be able to handle this information. That's why the top brass keep it quiet; they probably don't even brief the president completely."

I attend several lectures, and am impressed with how sincere, articulate and accomplished the speakers are. At one session a retired U.S. Air Force officer who has a degree in Aerospace Engineering from the Air Force Institute of Technology talks about the incident in which a UFO shut down eighteen Minuteman nuclear missiles at Malmstrom Air Force Base in 1967. One popular theory—popular in this group, at any rate—holds that the UFOs were most active in association with humanity's development of nuclear weapons, and that the space aliens were trying to keep us from engaging in nuclear warfare, knowing it would mean the end of our civilization. That's why there were so many sightings fifty years ago during the Cold War.

Of course there are many other questions about extraterrestrial life. And here at the MUFON conference, there are answers. In one session, an

Oxford-educated Rhodes Scholar finalist discusses possible reasons that the existence of extraterrestrial life has been covered up so completely. Many believe it is because alien spacecraft are powered by an almost-free energy source, and the military-industrial complex is doing everything it can to support the powerful oil industry—including suppression of the fact that there are alternative sources of energy.

My favorite session was a lecture by ... well, he asked me not to use his name outside the conference, so I'll call him Dr. Smith. "Just say I'm an Ivy League astrophysicist who works for the SETI [Search for Extraterrestrial Intelligence] Institute," Dr. Smith says. "There are plenty of us who fit that description; that will keep me anonymous enough."

Most of the other lecturers are retired, but not Dr. Smith. I'm astounded that he is willing to risk his reputation—and his Ivy League career, even though he's tenured—to explain for us the technology that he believes powers flying saucers. The doctor is in his mid-sixties and wears thick glasses with out-of-style frames and a brown tweed jacket with suede patches on the elbows. He looks the part a little too much, so I check him out online and find that he does indeed have a Ph.D. in astrophysics and he does work at an Ivy League university. He also has an affiliation with the Smithsonian. He's published more than 200 scientific papers—mostly in mainstream refereed journals—including one in *Scientific American* last month. The more I look, the more I'm impressed with his academic credentials.

Twenty minutes into Dr. Smith's presentation about quasars, black holes and the origin of the universe, it starts to get interesting. He has more than his own imagination to go on; he has interviewed several abductees who have described the interior of alien spaceships to him.

"When the spacecraft is operated by these alien beings, they're not pulling levers, or pressing pedals.... It is apparently their communal experience which is actually operating the spacecraft," Dr. Smith explains. To make a long explanation a bit shorter, the basic idea is that the magnetic quadrupole moment that results from the aliens' telepathic mind-meld is picked up by a highly hydrodynamically unstable—and therefore easily influenced—plasma field, which is "effectively generated by nature, but influenced by the communal, shared, telepathic experience of the four aliens that are guiding the spacecraft."

He'd said it: *Aliens*. This world-class astrophysicist was talking about alien beings. "Their hands fit into a glove-like structure and those gloves are what pick up that intentionality of theirs, and *that's* what is somehow amplified and magnified by that plasma power supply. That is apparently the driving power of the spacecraft." Dr. Smith pauses to let this information sink in: The aliens' intentionality is what powers the spacecraft. *No wonder the military-industrial complex doesn't want the information to get out,* I think. *Information like that would completely disrupt the world economy; it would cause unimaginable chaos.*

There's another part of the process: A crystal at the bottom of the spacecraft picks up the emanations from the plasma and leaks off a detritus that we experience as an excruciatingly bright light, which is the explanation for the very-bright-light-in-the-sky type of UFO—the kind Dad saw. There's also something about a quantum holographic projection that "achieves its gravity," an accomplishment that is impressive for a reason I don't quite grasp, and also neatly explains the seemingly bizarre flight patterns of spacecraft that appear to move instantaneously from one place to another—they are actually holograms appearing and disappearing, rather than actual physical objects moving around in space.

I'll admit I've lost the plot at this point. It must be an elegant theory that Dr. Smith is describing, though, because it is bringing together near-death experiences, the Higgs boson particle, co-spatial universes, magnetic frequency space, the Uncertainty Principle, God, time-travel and wormholes.

Dr. Smith continues, speaking carefully and qualifying nearly every thought with *apparently, probably, somehow, it seems*. For example, he suggests that "*probably*, we as conscious, sentient beings, are some kind of wormhole connection to the rest of the universe, and the experience of death is actually the closing of that wormhole."

All this is fascinating, but it's just too hard to keep up. Maybe if I'd listened more closely the day we covered wormholes in ... wait, *that's* the problem! I have no idea what a wormhole is. I look it up on my smartphone. "Like black holes, wormholes arise as valid solutions to the equations of Albert Einstein's General Theory of Relativity." No good. No help at all.

I try again; here's one: "A hypothetical connection between widely separated regions of space-time." That's a little better; it reminds me of the space-and-time-travel theory I read about years ago in Madeleine L'Engle's young adult novel, *A Wrinkle in Time*. She described it pretty well, and I drift off into a reverie, remembering the summer I read that book in my parents' backyard—the smells of mowed grass and the hot asphalt alleyway, and how thrilling it was to have come across such a unique and satisfying concept.

Forty minutes into his talk, Dr. Smith is explaining the relevance of quadrupole frequencies and shows a slide that gets my attention. It looks like this:

Phenomena and their Frequencies	
Frequency (Hz)	
1	Heartbeat, Sexual Intercourse, Rock-and-roll
2	
4	Sexual Practice (esp. masturbation), Rock-and-roll (4/4 time)
8	
16	Human Nervous System
32	
64	Power Grid (120 countries around the world)
128	
256	Middle C
512	
1024	Prana
2048	
4096	Prana

"The act of human sexual intercourse is centered at one hertz," Dr. Smith observes. "And when you think about it, the act of human intercourse is also the act that aligns the frequencies of two human beings to exact balance." I'm not sure how far the good doctor is planning to go with this, and I don't really want to be sitting next to my father during a lecture on human sexual intercourse.

Dr. Smith continues, "And it's also interesting that all rock-and-roll music ... is at one hertz." Rock-and-roll? I'm sure Dr. Smith will lose my father on this one, but I peek sideways and see that Dad is paying rapt attention.

Smith allows that he's been a little loose with the numbers—"The human heartbeat is not at *exactly* one hertz; it varies depending on whether you're awake or asleep"—but the general idea still works. Then Dr. Smith goes on to discuss the Grateful Dead, LSD, and "communal diddy-bopping at one hertz."

At this point I decide another quick reality check is in order, so I look up Middle C on my smartphone. The chart is pretty close: It's 261.1 hertz. We are nearing the end of Dr. Smith's presentation and he needs to wrap things up, so he skips explaining the prana part in favor of addressing a few more immediate issues.

Should we be worried? As if he'd anticipated my question—perhaps telepathically—Dr. Smith continues, "We know what the alien agenda is. They're here to work with us…. And I'm not alarmed at the mixing of DNA with aliens; I think we're already part of that mix…." *Already part of that mix? Is this distinguished astrophysicist saying we've been diddling with aliens?* My mind begins to spin.

As Dr. Smith's lecture draws to a close, I look around the room. Is anyone here "part of that mix"? How far does their "do not interfere" directive extend, and how is mixing with our DNA not part of it? Are there rogue aliens who do, indeed, interfere with humanity? Would I recognize an alien if I saw one?

The people around me do not seem like aliens, or like crackpots. Most appear to be intelligent, upstanding, accomplished people—maybe a little paranoid, but who wouldn't be, in their situation? They've had encounters they couldn't understand and couldn't talk about, experiences they could hardly even dare to think about without jeopardizing their careers and livelihoods. It's been a long day, but the people around me are energized.

Dad looks good, too. At seventy-nine, he is beginning to hunch his shoulders a little, but right now he's standing straight. His blue eyes sparkle, and there is a small, satisfied smile on his face. He is with his tribe. I'm glad I've come to the conference with Dad, although I'm not sure how long I'll last—this is only day one of a three-day symposium.

After dinner at a nearby restaurant Dad and I walk back to the hotel. Before entering the lobby we both pause and look up. We are scanning the night sky for a sign. I've seen Dad look up this same way on many occasions, but never really understood what he was looking for.

Now I do. It is a rare father-daughter moment, our own personal wormhole, a curiosity that will keep us connected—always—through time and space. From now on, I'll be looking up, too.

Reading Group
Discussion Questions

If You Enjoyed …
A Sneak Peek

Publication Notes

Resources

Acknowledgments

About the Author

Discussion Questions

1. What is the scariest thing you've ever done, and how did it affect you? Would you do it again? Why?

2. Is it our responsibility to try to help animals like kiwis and leatherback turtles survive? What about the Giant Gippsland Earthworms?

3. Are there incidents from your childhood—like watching *Wild Kingdom* on TV—that influenced you years later?

4. Would you like to try a chocolate massage? What sensual experience would you like to treat yourself to?

5. What is the most unusual food you've ever tried? Would you eat it again?

6. Lying, cheating, stealing, smuggling—are they always wrong? Why or why not?

7. If you could choose a different culture or religion to have grown up in, what would it be and why?

8. Do you think it's okay to use human body parts for research, such as developing an improved embalming technique like Frederic Ruysch did? Would you donate your body for research? Would you donate your organs to someone in need? Why or why not?

9. Do you think it's okay for scientists to create chimeras—creatures that combine genetic material from more than one species? (By the way, the FDA has approved the sale of salmon that is a chimera. It can grow to be more than ten times larger than a salmon that has not been genetically modified.)

10. Do you believe in UFOs? Do you know anyone who has seen one, or thinks they might have seen one? Do you believe extraterrestrial aliens might live among us?

Please do me a big favor and leave your comments on IndieBound.org, Amazon.com, and/or wherever you purchased your book.

Thanks very much!
—Laurie

IF YOU ENJOYED THESE STORIES

you might also like the ones in
Lost, Kidnapped, Eaten Alive!
True stories from a curious traveler.
It's my award-winning collection of
stories about adventures like these:

- Accidentally marrying
  a Maasai warrior.
- Being eaten alive by leeches.
- Studying French kissing in Paris.
- Tracking down the Balinese healer who
  befriended Elizabeth Gilbert in her bestselling
  book *Eat, Pray, Love.*

Publisher's Weekly said the book is "part cultural tour, part prayer to the natural world ... circles the globe with lively adventures and intimate insights."

Kirkus Reviews called it "an engaging, meticulously observed journey that brings other cultures alive." Other readers have called it witty, intelligent, savvy, quirky, fresh and fun.

Lost, Kidnapped, Eaten Alive! True stories from a curious traveler is available from your favorite bookseller.

To get you started, here's the chapter—OK *most* of the chapter—about being kidnapped ...

A Sneak Peek

from

Lost, Kidnapped, Eaten Alive!

True stories from a curious traveler

At a Crossroads

SOMEWHERE IN TUNISIA

I didn't know whether I was being kidnapped or rescued—that was what made my one big decision so difficult. That and the fact that I was young and foolish, and more than a little anxious about being stranded in the North African desert.

It all began quite innocently. Our bus had deposited Alan, my affable traveling companion, and myself at the door of a small, clean hotel in a dusty Tunisian village. The buildings were two stories high at most, covered with plaster, and whitewashed against the powdery red dust that enveloped the town and seemed to stretch forever. In the desperate heat of late afternoon, the place appeared to be completely deserted. Not a single shop was open and the dirt streets were empty: no vehicles, no pedestrians, not even a stray dog.

Inside, the 1940s-era hotel was as empty as the street. There were no brochures advertising nearby attractions (I suspected there *were* no nearby attractions); there was no "We accept VISA, MasterCard, and American Express" sign. That was okay; I had travelers' checks. There was no bouquet of silk flowers, no table, no couch on which weary travelers could rest. A lone white straight-backed chair stood sentry on the floor of exquisitely patterned blue and red ceramic tiles. The reception desk held a silver tray filled with mints.

I had only just met Alan, a wandering college student like myself, that morning. But I quickly decided he'd be great to travel with: he seemed friendly, calm and reasonable—not the type to freak out if a bus schedule changed or a train was delayed. Plus he spoke a little French, which I did not. Alan had a quick, cryptic conversation with the hotel clerk, and then translated for me. The clerk had pointed out that there were no taxis in the small town, and suggested that Alan hitch a ride to the local bar/restaurant—six miles out of town—for a beer and a bite to eat. It didn't occur to either of us that a woman shouldn't also venture out, and I was eager to see some sights, meet the locals, and have dinner. Of course I went along.

In retrospect, I realize I should have known better. We were in Tunisia, a country where women stay indoors and cover up like caterpillars in cocoons. The guidebooks had warned me to cover my shoulders and legs, and I felt quite modest and accommodating in a button-up shirt and baggy jeans.

When we arrived, I found that the place was more bar than restaurant, and that I was the only female present. Even the waiters were all men. But these details didn't seem important. After all, I had dressed conservatively, and decided to take the precaution—again, recommended by my guidebook—of avoiding direct eye contact with men. What could possibly go wrong?

Since I spoke neither French nor Arabic—and was assiduously avoiding eye contact—it was quite impossible for me to converse with anyone but Alan, who was busy putting his first-year college language skills to dubious use. I was bored. This was a plain-as-bread sort of establishment; there was no big screen TV soccer game, no video arcade, not even a friendly game of cards or a lively bar fight for me to watch. Just a lot of dark men in white robes, sitting in mismatched wooden chairs, speaking softly in a language I could not understand and drinking tiny cups of strong coffee. The bitter, familiar aroma was a meager comfort.

Then the music began; it sounded off-key and was startlingly loud and foreign—a little frightening, even. Next the belly dancers appeared: twelve gorgeous women, one after another, with long, dark hair, burnished skin, flowing diaphanous skirts in brilliant vermilion and aqua and emerald, gold necklaces, belts, bracelets, anklets. Gold everywhere: tangled cords jangling against long brown necks; fine, weightless strands decorating the swirling fabrics; heavy gold chains slapping in a satisfying way against ample abdominal flesh. They were a remarkable contrast to the stark room and simple furnishings, and I began to realize that things in Tunisia were not entirely as they first appeared.

The music quickened, and the dancers floated across the bar—which had somehow been converted into a stage—and around the room, weaving in and out among tables, lingering occasionally for a long glance at a pleased patron. Soon they were at our table, looking not at Alan but at me, urging me, with their universal body language, to join them.

Did I dare? My stomach clenched momentarily. I knew my dancing would be clumsy and ugly next to theirs, my short-cropped hair and lack of makeup un-attractively boyish, my clothing shapeless and without style or significant color. I wore no jewelry— as the guidebook suggested—just my glasses, which were not particularly flattering.

Of course I am relatively unattractive and clumsy

256

A Sneak Peek

in this foreign environment, I thought, *but there is no need to be priggish as well.* And the women were by now insistent, actually taking me by both hands and pulling me up to dance with them. Flushed with embarrassment, I did my best to follow their swaying hips and graceful arm movements as we made our way around the room once again. Even with the aid of the two beers, I was not foolish enough to attempt to duplicate their astonishing abdominal undulations.

As soon as I thought these exotic, insistent beauties would allow it, I broke the line and resumed my place—plain, awkward, very white, and completely out of my element—next to Alan. Thereafter, it was excruciatingly embarrassing for me to watch the dancers, and Alan agreed to accompany me back to the hotel. He, too, had had enough excitement for the evening and was ready to retire, so he asked the bartender to call us a cab. A fellow bar patron overheard the conversation and was kind enough to offer us a lift. The man wore Western-style clothing, understood Alan's French, and seemed safe enough; we felt fortunate to have arranged the ride in spite of our limited linguistic abilities and the fact that the night was still young.

But that's when the evening turned ugly. Two well-dressed, middle-aged men left the bar immediately after we did. We saw them get into a black Mercedes, and we watched in the rear-view mirror as they trailed us, just our car and theirs, bumping along a sandy road in the empty desert. There were no buildings, streetlights or pedestrians, and we saw no other vehicles.

I looked out the window, enjoying the vast, black night sky and trying to ignore my growing sense of anxiety. When we came to an unmarked Y inter-section, our driver, in a bizarrely ineffective attempt at deception, headed steadily towards the road on the right, then veered off at the last second to take the road on the left. Neither Alan nor I could remember which direction we'd come from hours earlier, when it was still light out and we were not under the spell of Tunisian music and belly dancers and beer. The strange feigning and last-second careening alarmed us both.

And it got worse. Immediately after the incident at the intersection, the men in the car behind us revved the engine, chased us down and ran us off the road and into a ditch. They stood in the road, shouting and gesticulating wildly outside our car. My hands went icy in the warm night air. Despite—or perhaps because of—an imposing language barrier, we had the impression that the men who ran our car off the road were attempting to rescue us.

But what, exactly, were they rescuing us from? Was our driver a sociopathic kidnapper bent on selling us into slavery? A rapist? A murderer? And why were our "rescuers" so insistent? Was it out of the goodness of their hearts, or did they, too, have some sinister motive? We had to make a choice. One car would probably take us safely to our hotel; the other might lead to a terrifying fate. But we had no idea which was which.

In this moment of crisis, we clenched hands and Alan looked at me—somewhat desperately, I thought—for a decision. I tried to assess his strength, and wondered whether he was a good fighter. (Probably not—he was a Yale man.) My stomach churned, but I forced myself to concentrate. We had only two options: We could remain in the long black limo, hope it could be extricated from the ditch, and hope our volunteer driver really was the kind and innocuous man he had appeared to be.

Or we could bolt from the car, scramble out of the ditch, and as quickly as possible, put our rescuers and their car between ourselves and the man who had so generously offered us a ride. The two men were still shouting, and began to pound and slap the driver's window. Even so, Alan leaned towards staying. After all, he reasoned, it was only one man, and there were two of us. Surely we could overpower him and escape if it proved necessary.

I wanted to bolt. Even though there were two men in the "rescue" car, as opposed to only one in our vehicle, I had become certain, in some wholly subjective way, that our man was crazy, and I'd heard that crazy people can be quite strong. Plus, our apparent rescuers, the men who had just run us off the road, warned Alan that we were with "*un homme méchant! mauvais!*"—a wicked man. But the deciding factor was that these two men had actually gone to the trouble of following us out of the bar, chasing us down, running our car off the road and into a dusty ditch, and were now expending a great deal of energy trying to convince us of something.

Surely that constellation of actions bespoke a serious purpose, such as rescuing two foolish young travelers from a lifetime of misery in the North African desert. The two men must be rescuers; kidnappers were not likely to go to so much trouble, or to risk scratching or even denting their shiny black late-model Mercedes in the process.

Alan was no help; I had to make a decision myself, and quickly. But what about the downside? In the middle of all the commotion—and with Alan sitting next to me looking more than a little uncertain— I realized that we had not yet fully considered the

A Sneak Peek

potential negative consequences of an incorrect choice. If we chose to stay, and it was the wrong choice, the man would undoubtedly drive us to some sort of central kidnapping headquarters—probably an impenetrable, fortress-like stone building with dark, echoing corridors, or perhaps a sweltering, waterless hovel cleverly hidden in remote, sand-swept dunes. In that case, he would have a knife, or a gun, or evil partners—or perhaps all of the above—and the fact that the two of us probably could have overpowered him would be moot. We would be goners.

On the other hand, if we bolted, and that was the wrong choice, we would be double-goners because the two men could also turn out to be kidnappers or murderers who could easily overpower us. Downsides being equally awful, we decided to go with our gut. Or guts. The problem was that Alan's gut said stay, and mine said bolt....

―――――――

I hope you've enjoyed the beginning of "At a Crossroads." To find out whether or not I made it out alive, you can read the entire story—plus twenty-two others—in *Lost, Kidnapped, Eaten Alive! True stories from a curious traveler*, available from your favorite bookseller.

Publication Notes

Many of these essays, or similar versions of them, have previously been published elsewhere:

A version of "At a Crossroads" was first published in *The Kindness of Strangers* (Lonely Planet, 2003), edited by Don George and with a preface by His Holiness the Dalai Lama.

"Cheater's High" was published in *Wandering in Cornwall: Mystery, Mirth and Transformation in the Land of the Ancient Celts* (Wanderland Writers, 2015).

"Chocotherapy" was published in *Wandering in Andalusia: The Soul of Southern Spain* (Wanderland Writers, 2016).

"Finding my Inner Gypsy" was published in *Wandering in Andalusia: The Soul of Southern Spain* (Wanderland Writers, 2016).

A version of "The Ghosts on Angel Island" was published in *Marin* magazine in September, 2016 with the title "Ellis Island of the West."

"Hooked on Hawk Hill" was published in *Marin* magazine in July, 2017.

A version of "Lucky Sama" was published on Medium.com in 2016. The story won the international Planet Earth Gold Award for 2017, for Best Travel Article or Essay for Planet Earth.

"The Mermaid, the Curmudgeon, the Magician, and the Churchyard" was published in *Wandering in Cornwall: Mystery, Mirth and Transformation in the Land of the Ancient Celts* (Wanderland Writers, 2015).

About the Cover Image:

Those of you who are clever about such things will have noticed that the reptile head on the cover is that of an alligator, not a crocodile. I needed a cover image, happened to have an alligator head around the house (it was a gift), and decided it would be an acceptable substitute for the crocodile head I did not have, given that this is not a scientific treatise. The alligator was not killed for this purpose, nor would I have harmed any vertebrate in the service of a cover shot.

About the Ouroboros Image:

In Ancient Greek, ouroboros means *tail-devouring*. I'm captivated by the image—a serpent swallowing its own tail, being created through its own destruction.

The symbol's meaning is nearly as varied as the many cultures that have embraced it over millennia, but there's a beautiful unity in what it represents: regeneration, reincarnation, immortality, the cycle of life and death, the harmony of opposites, the eternal unity of all things, perpetuity and infinity.

The image used here is after a woodcut in a 1760 book titled *Uraltes Chymisches Werck von Abraham Eleazar*, or the *Age Old Chemical Work of Abraham Eleazar*.

Resources

- The **Angel Island Immigration Station,** where I found out about "The Ghosts on Angel Island—https://www.aiisf.org/

- **Din Tai Fung,** where I learned the secrets of "The Dumpling Men of Taipei—http://dintaifungusa.com/

- **The Fortress of the Bear** where I met Chaik, Killisnoo, and the other characters in "Prayer Bear— http://www.fortressofthebear.org/

- **Golden Gate Raptor Observatory** (GGRO) where I learned to band hawks and got "Hooked on Hawk Hill"— http://www.parksconservancy.org/programs/ggro/

- The **Kunstkamera** (or Kunstkammer) where Peter the Great displayed items from "The Cabinet of Curiosities"— http://www.kunstkamera.ru/en/

- The **Mutual UFO Network** (MUFON) that organized the conference described in "They've Seen the Saucers"— http://www.mufon.com/

- **Nature Seekers,** who help educate the public and protect the leatherback turtles in "Leatherback Love"— http://www.natureseekers.org/

- **Pinawalla Elephant Orphanage,** where "Lucky Sama" lives— https://lanka.com/about/attractions/pinnawala-elephant-orphanage/

- **SkyWalk,** where you can test your own "Fear of Not Flying"—http://skywalk.co.nz/

- **Sri Dalada Maligawa,** where I visited "The Temple of the Tooth"—http://www.sridaladamaligawa.lk/

Acknowledgments

With deep appreciation for Joanna Biggar, who edited several of the stories in this collection, Linda Watanabe McFerrin, who edited almost all the rest, and the members of Linda's Advanced Writers Workshop, whose thoughtful and patient critiques—and inspiring craftmanship—motivated me to finish the book.

And with endless gratitude to Jim Shubin, The Book Alchemist, for editorial help, ongoing encouragement, and a cover I absolutely adore.

About the Author

Laurie McAndish King grew up in rural Iowa, studied philosophy and science at Cornell College, and has traveled to forty countries. She observes with an eye for natural science, and writes with a philosopher's heart and mind.

Laurie's award-winning travel essays and photography have appeared in many publications, including *Smithsonian* magazine, Travel Channel affiliate iExplore.com, Travelers' Tales' *The Best Women's Travel Writing*, and others. Her writing has won a Lowell Thomas gold award and her mobile app about the San Francisco Waterfront earned a 5-star rating on iTunes.

Laurie's first travel memoir, *Lost, Kidnapped, Eaten Alive! True stories from a curious traveler*, was published in 2014 and won four literary awards.

Laurie also wrote *An Erotic Alphabet* (for which she was dubbed "The Shel Silverstein of Erotica") and co-edited two volumes in the *Hot Flashes: Sexy little stories & poems* series. She is an avid photographer—one of her photos was displayed at the Smithsonian—and enjoys gardening, taxidermy, and, on occasion, chasing the cosmic serpent.

Her website is www.LaurieMcAndishKing.com.

53448511R00165

Made in the USA
San Bernardino, CA
18 September 2017